Best Vegan Recipes

1st edition
ISBN 978-0-9936996-0-3
Printed in Canada
Best-Vegan.com

FSC
www.fsc.org
MIX
Paper from
responsible sources
FSC® C016245

Thank you

My incredible family has been so supportive in helping this book come alive. Thanks to my Mum and Dad, Step-mum Gerry, Uncle Ken, Auntie Ruth, brother Cam, and Granny. You are the most amazing family! Thanks also to Dirk Slot for his talented film and photography contributions to my projects and to this book. Many thanks to the wonderful restaurants in *Best Vegan Recipes* who have made this book come together with the tastiest recipes around!

Edible Contents

Appetizers

Breakfasts

Desserts

Edible Contents

Entrées

Pasta Sauces

Sides and Snacks

Edible Contents

Sauces, Spreads, Dips & Dressings

Smoothies

Soups

Edible Contents

Salads

Raw Foods

North American Restaurant Tour

Introduction

My passion for a vegan diet transpired in my early 20s when I learned of the abuse factory farmed animals endure, the effects animal production have on the environment and the drain it causes on the global food supply. From this I decided being a vegan was the best thing I could do for the world. I volunteered with PETA, wrote articles on veganism and started to promote a healthy, plant-based diet.

When I began eating a plant-based diet I was at the start of a six-month tour around the United States. I absolutely adored going to vegan and live food restaurants and getting to know the staff and owners. When I was at home I wanted to cook food that was as delicious as the meals at these restaurants. I bought recipe books and used my imagination to try to recreate my favorite restaurant items. I had a dinner party every Sunday where we would all make vegan and live food and take it home for the week. (I highly recommend this. It's a fun way to organize your food for the week and learn how to cook new recipes.)

I spent this time cooking and researching restaurants because I wanted to create a cookbook filled with exceptional vegan recipes. Well, one thing led to another and over time the idea came to me. If I wanted the best vegan recipes, I needed to go straight to the source: top vegan restaurants in North America.

So, with the idea came a huge project. Hundreds of hours of research, coupled with a lot of advice and direction from some of the industry's top chefs, critics and restaurateurs. That research brought about hundreds of hours of traveling, visits to many different restaurants and heaps and heaps of incredible eating.

The restaurants that were chosen are North America's top rated vegan restaurants I was directed to by respected industry professionals, vegan groups and media sources and then I approved them because of their incredible food. You will find the restaurants have reviews, reputations and often awards that demonstrate a general consensus that they are North America's best.

The restaurants include high-end, five star restaurants and simple diners that will blow your mind. The majority of the restaurants are completely vegan, some are live food restaurants, and others don't have an entirely vegan menu but are famous for their vegan options. Many of the restaurants have wonderful atmospheres, friendly staff, agreeable prices and so forth, but it is the food that has been critiqued and is amazing and supreme.

After the restaurants were chosen I started collecting recipes. I asked the restaurant owners to send customer favorites and to avoid overly complicated recipes. I also told them I prefer healthy recipes, yet the only necessity was that they are exceptionally tasty!

I cooked them all and had a lot of happy friends willing to sample them. I became an incredible vegan cook through this experience, and that is what I want for you, the reader: to really use this book.

Every recipe in Best Vegan Recipes is outstanding and this book can turn you into an exceptional vegan cook, giving you the ability to make recipes that will impress anyone. If you are already an excellent vegan chef it will give you a host of new recipes and introduce creative ideas from top chefs across the continent.

For new cooks I recommend you start with simple recipes and take on the more complicated selections as you go. After you have cooked the recipe once, repeats are much easier. Below the recipe title there is a guide including the level of difficulty between 1 and 5, 1 being the simplest. I recommend new cooks stick with recipes in the 1 to 3 range. The guide also states if recipes are gluten-free (G/F) and / or soy-free (S/F).

When I started, I felt overwhelmed by many of the recipes I was cooking. Now I have most of the spices and base ingredients on hand, and I know what I am doing. Even the complicated ones seem comparatively simple to the first recipes I cooked. I find cooking to be a wonderful way to relax and escape the daily grind. I like to turn on some music, light some candles and create something exceptional!

I hope you enjoy the book and use it well. I wish to proposition you with a challenge, and if you accept this challenge the result will be that you become an exceptional, diverse and knowledgeable vegan cook.

The challenge: take the next two years to cook a new recipe from Best Vegan Recipes once a week. You will have cooked the entire book by the end of this journey, which will have turned you into a amazing vegan cook. This will give you a wealth of recipes to recreate any time you wish. I promise friends, lovers and family will adore your new skills! As you build up your spice cupboard and savory shopping skills, the recipes will become much less expensive to make. During this time you will find your absolute favorite recipes and ones that are simple and inexpensive to recreate regularly.

Whether you are a vegan or just want to eat more vegan food you may as well spend your life as a skilled cook eating amazing meals!

Today I continue making delicious vegan food and teaching others through my cooking classes. I live in Victoria, British Columbia, Canada and travel North America teaching, eating and continuing to learn. I am full of gratitude for each of the restaurants in Best Vegan Recipes for their contributions to this book and for giving us the opportunity to create recipes from top vegan chefs. One can view pictures, new recipes and my upcoming cooking classes at best-vegan.com

Bon Appetit!

Juice Feast Detox Retreat

Today's world is full of toxins from the air to the water to the emotional toxins our bodies hold in from the stresses of life. The toxins age our bodies from the inside out, cause health problems, can lead to water retention and weight gain and disturb our mental clarity and emotional well-being. I did not realize how affected we are from toxics that reside in our bodies until I started Juice Feasting to cleanse.

Juice Feasting is a program of abundance where the participants drink 3 to 4 liters of fresh organic juice daily, along with liquefied super foods. As a result of my own and close friend Tyler Twiss' incredible results with Juice Feasting we decided to host a Juice Feasting Detox Retreat on Vancouver Island, in the warmest part of Canada.

At the retreat, fresh, organic fruit and vegetable juices are served all day, along with hot teas and liquified super foods. Each guest has a their own room and bathroom in a lovely countryside resort.

Here we offer an optional daily schedule with a variety of classes, including yoga and art, and positive cinema at night. There is pampering and time for a guest to relax with massage and use the detoxing infrared sauna and salt water hot tub. Juice is continually available. Not a lot of eating goes on here, but guests still don't go hungry!

The results are complete rejuvenation. Guests leave glowing, refreshed, revived and on a healthier path.

My partner Tyler Twiss and I choose the Juice Feasting cleansing program because it includes 12 to 15 pounds of organic fruits and vegetables that are juiced daily along with super foods. This gives participants the nutrition their bodies crave and a rest for their digestive systems. While a person is on a liquid diet their bodies naturally and rapidly start to pump out toxins. Most of the body's energy is used digesting foods; on a cleanse the body turns energy to healing ailments and preventing future illness.

Along with the cleanse, patrons are given the tools, classes and techniques to eliminate these toxins permanently. Guests stay an average of 3 to 10 days.

This program helps with weight issues, mental clarity, a youthful appearance, energy level, a positive outlook and much more. The results are truly incredible.

Tyler and I had a great response from the first retreat we hosted and have developed a loyal following. The Juice Feasting Detox Retreat continues to grow and I am constantly inspired by the immediate and long-term changes that guests experience.

juicefeastretreat.com

"Juice Feasting with Tyler and Jamie has been an experience of nourishment and abundance. I am grateful for their unstinting loving-kindness, their impeccable support. I thoroughly enjoyed the peaceful and gracious atmosphere of the H' Bay Retreat and look forward to my next Juice Feast Retreat."

~ Maryam WexlerW

"I felt incredible during and after the juice feast retreat. My only regret was that I did not stay longer. I can't wait for the next one."

Heather Black

"I went on vacation to get away from things but could not believe the incredible life changing experience I found. In a week I lost 14 pounds, increased my energy and improved my attitude. I have not felt so healthy in decades and continue a healthier life style today. I will be back next year!"

~Ken McGill

juicefeastretreat.com

Vast sun-drenched deserts

seem unchanged until they are splashed with the beautiful desert rain. Prickly cactus's bloom bright flowers and

the sweetest oranges grow out of this heated land.

Arizona's hot summers help make citrus sweet, chilies spicy and dates ripe.

Fresh Mint

Fresh Mint is a bright, happy and casual restaurant that boasts extraordinary vegan cuisine with a Vietnamese spin. The restaurant perfected its recipes during the 10 years it was located in Hawaii. Fresh Mint opened a location in Scottsdale, Arizona in 2008 and has found a host of new fans in the area. At the Arizona location, visitors listen to beach music in a room with splashy green and purple walls adorned with Asian art work and the largest mint leaf replica you will ever see. It is a family owned and run business where you will often find the daughter, wife and husband there to help you.

Chef, mother and wife Mai Ly has mastered the flavors of spices, herbs and special ingredients that leave Fresh Mint recipes so very tasty. Everything is made fresh when ordered so it tastes its best. The menu has a nice selection of appetizers, salads, soups, noodle dishes, entrées and desserts. Most items are vegan and all items are vegetarian. The creative talents of Fresh Mint can be tasted through the Fresh Mint Tomato Delight recipe. This is a comforting entrée composed of fried tomatoes bursting with creamy tofu, wonderful chanterelle mushrooms, carrots and noodles. The Curry Apple Tofu recipe is a great demonstration of the Hawaiian and Asian flare that Fresh Mint does so well. It is sweetened with apple cranberry, is made creamy with coconut milk and rendered spiced with curry. These are lovely dishes that let each of us taste the excellent creative flavors of Fresh Mint.

"Best Vegetarian" *Arizona Foothills Magazine* "Healthy Plates" Fresh Mint Featured ~ PHOENIX Magazine **"Passport to Asia"** Fresh Mint Featured ~ PHOENIX Magazine "85 Best Restaurants" Fresh Mint Featured ~ PHOENIX Magzine **"10 Veggie Virtuosos"** **Fresh Mint Listed #1 ~** *The Arizona Republic* "Top 100 Favorite Dishes 2011" Fresh Mint Featured "Kung Pao Soy Chicken ~ *Phoenix New Times* "Best Vegetarian Restaurant" ~ *Phoenix New Times* **"10 Super Foods for Better Health"** **Fresh Mint Listed #1 ~** *The Arizona Republic* "Top 5 Dining Picks This Weekend" Fresh Mint Listed # 1 Scottsdale Republic "20 Spots For Chow That's Good and Good For You" Fresh Mint Featured ~ *AZ Weekly Magazine* **"Restaurants Taking Heed of Herbivores" Fresh Mint Listed # 1** ~ Scottsdal Republic

"The soul should always stand ajar, ready to welcome the ecstatic experience."

Emily Dickinson

Tomato Delight

(Stuffed Pan-Fried Tomatoes)
Fresh Mint

Preparation time: 30 minutes ~ Serves: 8 ~ Level of difficulty: 3 ~ Equipment: Non-stick frying pan - G/F

This is a fantastic recipe that is light, warm and flavorful. Creamy tofu mixed with wonderful shiitake mushrooms, carrots, onions and noodles bulge out of a fried tomato. It is a delight!

Ingredients

2 teaspoons vegetable oil, divided
50 grams bean vermicelli, available at Asian markets
1/2 cup onion, small diced
1 cup carrot, finely diced
3 large shiitake mushrooms, small diced
1 14-ounce package of firm tofu
salt and pepper

8 medium firm ripe tomatoes
4 teaspoons green onion, finely chopped
2 teaspoons mushroom powder (found in Asian markets, or make your own by grinding dried mushrooms in a spice grinder or coffee grinder)

Method

1. In a small bowl, soak the vermicelli in cool water for five minutes until it is slightly soft and easy to cut.
2. Drain the water and dice the vermicelli into small pieces. Set aside.
3. In the pan, heat 1 teaspoon of the vegetable oil on medium-high heat. Add the onion and stir until it is soft.
4. Add the carrot, shiitake mushrooms, prepared vermicelli and one teaspoon of the mushroom powder. Sauté until the vegetables are soft. Set aside in a separate dish.
5. Pat the tofu dry with a paper towel and then crumble into small pieces.
6. Add the tofu to the pan and sauté on medium heat for five minutes. Season with salt and pepper to taste and stir well. Remove from heat and combine with the prepared vegetables.
7. Cut the tomatoes in half, and scoop out the insides. Dice the insides into small pieces and set aside.
8. Fill the halved tomatoes with the prepared tofu and vegetable mix.
9. Heat the remaining vegetable oil on medium and carefully add the filled tomatoes. Cook until the bottoms are golden. Set on plates.
10. In the same pan, heat the diced tomato insides and the remaining mushroom powder. Pour over the stuffed tomatoes.
11. Garnish with green onion and serve immediately with a side of your favorite raw or steamed vegetables.

Curry Apple Tofu
Fresh Mint

Preparation time: 45 minutes ~ Cook time: 15 minutes ~ Serves: 2 ~ Level of difficulty: 2.5 ~ Equipment: 12-inch non-stick skillet ~ G/F

This flavorful dish is spiced with curry, sweetened with apple and made creamy with warm tofu and coconut milk.

Ingredients

2 teaspoons vegetable oil

2 teaspoon curry powder

1 teaspoon sugar

1/2 teaspoon salt

12 ounces tofu, drained, patted dry and cut into 3/4-inch cubes

1 medium green apple, cut into 3/4-inch cubes

1/2 of a yellow onion, cut into 1/8-inch slices

2 shallots, thinly sliced

1 medium tomato, cut into 3/4-inch cubes

1/4 cup coconut milk

1 tablespoon dried sweetened cranberries

2 teaspoons mushroom powder (optional)

2 tablespoons roasted cashews, chopped, divided

Optional - your favorite vegetable to serve with Curry Apple Tofu

Method

1. Combine curry, sugar and salt in a bowl. Add the tofu cubes and green apple and turn to coat them evenly. Marinate for 30 minutes.
2. Heat 1 teaspoon of the oil in the skillet over medium-high heat. Add the onion and shallots and stir until fragrant, about 1 minute. Reduce the heat to low and cook until the onions are soft, about 3 minutes. Transfer to a plate and keep warm.
3. Wipe the pan clean and heat the remaining oil over medium heat. Add the tofu mixture and, using chopsticks or wooden spoons, turn so it cooks evenly, about 4 to 5 minutes. Add the onion mixture and cook, uncovered, for another 2 minutes.
4. Add the tomato cubes and coconut milk and simmer another minute. Add cranberry, mushroom powder and 1 tablespoon of the cashews, mixing well.
5. Remove from the heat and transfer to a serving plate. Garnish with the remaining cashews and serve immediately with vegetables of choice.

Lovin' Spoonfuls

Restaurant owner Peggy Raisglid walked into a seminar a carnivore on August 14, 1989 and after hearing a speech detailing the abuse of farmed animals she walked out a vegan. Over the next decade she became well known by her friends for her great vegan food. People's admiration of her food eventually prompted her to open an entirely vegan restaurant: Lovin' Spoonfuls.

Peggy says the name describes the restaurant perfectly. She explains there is love that goes into each spoonful of food, love for the animals, love for the people they serve and love for the food.

Crispy Golden Nuggets, Bacon Cheeseburgers with large patties and heaps of cheese, Classic Turkey Sandwiches, and Sweet Creamy Banana Crème Pie—this menu goes beyond a vegan's dream but it is all plant-based food, which is delicious!

The restaurant has received heaps of media attention and awards for its exceptional food. Lovin' Spoonfuls is an unpretentious and casual place, which has kept its prices low for patrons. The restaurant stays full of happy customers and continues to serve with a lot of Love!

"Lovin' Spoonfuls Vegetarian Restaurant, where every spoonful is made with love."

Restaurant owner, Peggy Raisglid

Best Of Tucson
2006, 2007, 2008, 2009, 2010, 2011, 2012
Tucson Weekly

Top Vegetarian Restaurant
VegNews Magazine

Gold Award Winner
2007, 2008, 2009, 2010, 2011, 2012, 2013
Tucson Lifestyle Magazine

**Best Vegan Pie Top 5
National Award**
PETA

"Love is always the answer to healing of any sort." ~ Louise Hay

Banana Crème Pie

Lovin' Spoonfuls

Preparation time: 35 minutes ~ Serves: 8 ~ Level of difficulty: 3

This Banana Cream Pie was chosen by PETA as one of the top five desserts in the country and has received national and local recognition. You can taste why: the crust is soft and filled with a delightful creamy banana pie filling layered with wonderful soft whipped crème. Sweet and delightful!

Ingredients

8-inch organic, whole wheat pie shell
I box vegan whipped cream (SoyaToo brand and Mimic-Creme both work well; canned style is not recommended)
1/4 cup corn starch
3/4 cup organic, unrefined sugar

1 1/2 cups unsweetened soy milk
3 tablespoons organic, non-hydrogenated margarine
2 teaspoons real vanilla extract
2 ripe bananas
chopped walnuts to sprinkle on top of pie

Method

1. Bake the 8-inch organic, whole wheat pie shell until golden and set aside to cool.
2. Whip the box of vegan whipped cream. Set aside to chill.
3. In a sauce pan combine the corn starch and sugar. While stirring, slowly add 1/4 cup of the soy milk, and mix until smooth. Mix in the remaining soy milk and blend until smooth.
4. Heat the mixture in the sauce pan until it thickens and is just starting to bubble. Remove from heat.
5. Add the margarine and vanilla. Stir to combine.
6. Cool the filling completely. Fold in a 1/2 cup of the vegan whipped cream.
7. Line the pie shell with two sliced ripe bananas, and pour the filling over top. Decorate with vegan whipped cream and chopped walnuts.

Beautiful British Columbia,

Vancouver B.C.

Breakwater Pier at Ogden Point, Victoria, B.C.

Canada

Vineyards in Kelowna, B.C.

Cafe Bliss

Cafe Bliss is located in my hometown, Victoria, British Columbia, which makes me... blissful. The restaurant is a happy, friendly place to visit. The restaurant has a simple layout with large front-facing windows and earthy art and inspirational quotes are painted on the walls. The food is always healthy and mostly raw, which makes it energizing and uplifting. This is why Cafe Bliss is my standby place to go if I ever need a lift.

Heather, the owner, is a sweet soul who uses her thoughtful ways to inspire her staff to work from the heart. The restaurant is all about love. Heather makes the food with love and treats people in a loving way. Her loving influence is demonstrated through the kind and caring staff. She has recently opened a second location called Be Love located at 1019 Blanshard St, in Victoria. It is a full service restaurant offering a similar menu to Bliss with more cooked options.

Cafe Bliss was created to serve nourishing food that tastes delicious, is pristinely healthy and is "100% made with love." Energizing and healthful ingredients are combined in tasty, creative ways. The restaurant uses organic, mostly raw, plant source ingredients selected according to seasonal and local availability.

Raw and cooked entrées and decadent raw desserts are complemented by a wide variety of juices. The raw desserts are incredible; I am hooked on the Breakfast Brownie and Bliss Kiss. Both are small chocolate treats that are packed with sweet nutrition.

The Cafe Bliss recipes we have been gifted with—the Yogi Wrap and Wild Raw Tomato Soup— will pamper your taste buds and feed your mind, body and soul.

Follow your Bliss.

Wild Raw Tomato Soup
Cafe Bliss

Level of difficulty: 3 ~ Prep time 10 min after soaking sun-dried tomatoes for 30 min ~ Serves: 4 ~ Equipment: Blender ~ G/F & S/F

A note from Cafe Bliss:
Stinging nettles grow abundantly in the Pacific Northwest and can be harvested in the spring. They are high in iron and many trace minerals and are an incredible source of nutrition. They are used medicinally for women's health, inflammation and as a blood purifier. They have a strong green flavor that is excellent with tomatoes.

Ingredients

4 medium ripe tomatoes
1 cup fresh nettle tops
1/2 cup sun-dried tomatoes, soaked for half an hour
1/2 cup hemp hearts
1 teaspoon salt

1/4 cup fresh basil (or 2 teaspoons dried)
1 teaspoon ground black pepper
1 clove garlic
4 cups hot water

Method

1. Blend all ingredients in a high-speed blender until smooth.
2. Garnish with fresh basil leaves, chopped parsley or hemp hearts. Serve immediately.

"It is not how much we do...
but how much love we put in
that action."

Mother Teresa

Yogi Wraps

Coconut Curry Collard Wrap with Apple Mint Chutney
Cafe Bliss

In Advance: Soak cashews for at least six hours. Soak raisins for at least four hours. ~ Preparation time: 40 minutes ~ Serves: 4-6 ~ Level of difficulty: 3 ~ Equipment: Food processor ~ G/F

Yogi wraps are one of my favorite healthy meals. They are a perfect combination of healthful ingredients that come together to make an exotic and flavorful meal. They contain a delightful flavor combination with the spiciness of coconut curry paste, brightened with fresh veggies and balanced by brown rice. The Apple Mint Chutney adds the perfect sweetness to flatter these exotic wraps. Get ready to feel grounded, revived and healthy.

Ingredients

For the Coconut Curry Pate:
1 cup carrot, chopped
1 cup cashews, soaked
1/4 cup purified water
1/4 of a small red onion, chopped
1 large date, pitted
3 tablespoons miso
2 tablespoons lime juice
1 tablespoon fresh ginger
1 tablespoon curry powder
1/2 teaspoon salt
1/4 teaspoon black pepper
1/4 teaspoon turmeric
1 cup dried shredded coconut

For the Apple Mint Chutney:
2 apples, chopped
1/2 cup raisins, soaked
1/4 cup fresh mint leaves
1/4 of a jalapeño pepper with seeds
2 tablespoon apple cider vinegar
1/4 teaspoon salt

For the Blanched Collard Wraps:
8-12 large collard leaves or 16-24 small or medium size collard leaves
4 cups brown rice, cooked
2 cups cabbage, shredded
1 red bell pepper, sliced into strips
4 cups sprouts

Method

For the Coconut Curry Pate:
1. Place all ingredients except the dried coconut in the food processor. Process until smooth.
2. Add the coconut and process to just mix. Place in the fridge.

For the Apple Mint Chutney:
1. Place all ingredients in the food processor and process to a slightly chunky consistency. Place in the fridge.

For the Blanched Collard Wraps:
1. Cut the thick part of the stem from the bottom of the leaves.
2. Place the leaves in a large bowl and pour enough boiling water over them to cover them. Let them sit in the hot water for 1 to 3 minutes.
3. Remove the leaves one at a time and dry them with a clean towel.

Assembly

1. Place one large or two small blanched collard leaves on a hard surface with the outside of the leaf down and the bottom of the leaf closest to you. If you are using two smaller leaves, overlap them.
2. Place 1/4 cup of curry pate on the leaf near the bottom and pat it down along the length of the leaf leaving one or two inches of leaf on either side for folding in the sides.
3. Place 1/3 cup of rice on top of the pate and pat it down following the shape of the pate. Evenly distribute 1/4 cup of shredded cabbage, 2 or 3 slices of red pepper and one large handful sprouts on the leaf.
4. Fold in the sides and roll up your wrap. Cut the wrap in half diagonally and serve with Apple Mint Chutney on the side for dipping.

Feeding Change

> "Our vision is to reconnect us back to the food we eat and help us understand how it impacts our health, how it impacts our planet's health, and how it is connected to poverty, hunger, global warming, deforestation, water contamination and many other social issues we are faced with today" Preet Marwaha

Preet Marwaha, owner of Feeding Change, is a man impassioned and dedicated to caring for our earth and he has built his business to support this drive. One of Preet's restaurant, Organic Lives, closed due to a fire but new doors will be opening in the future under the name Feeding Change. I could not keep these tasty recipes from Organic Lives out of this book: the bright, fresh Raw Tortilla Soup and sweet, creamy Strawberry Blonde Smoothie.

Today Preet works as an instructor at the Institute of Holistic Nutrition and Organic Lives Education Centre. He also performs public health talks for schools and corporations. Preet has been involved globally on numerous projects including the World Wellness Project, Safe Planet Campaign and the United Nations Environment Programme (UNEP). He is focused on his new business, Feeding Change, and the mission is to "cultivate healthy, inspired and just communities by producing and supplying the purest, most nutrient-rich and delicious food, sourcing ingredients from pristine ecosystems and closely nurturing respectful relationships from soil to soul." May we all be fed and inspired by the healthful and dedicated work of

Preet Marwaha.

Strawberry Blonde Smoothie

Feeding Change

Yeilds: 1 16 ounce serving ~ Preparation time: 10 minutes ~ Level of difficulty: 1 ~ Equipment: Vita-Mix or other blender ~ G/F & S/F

Creamy coconut, a hint of vanilla twisted with pineapple, banana and strawberry flavors. This smoothie is perfectly delicious!

Ingredients

1 cup coconut milk
1/3 cup strawberries, fresh or frozen
1/2 cup pineapple, chopped
1/8 teaspoon vanilla
1 banana, frozen

Tip: add a splash of almond milk if you would like your smoothie to be thinner.

Method

1. In a Vita-Mix or other blender, blend all of the ingredients until smooth but still thick. Do not over blend.

Raw Tortilla Soup
Feeding Change

In advance: Soak brazil nuts for 4 hours or over night. Prepare soup, then let the diced garnish macerate in the base broth for 1-2 hours ~ Preparation time: 30 minutes
Serves: 4 ~ Level of difficulty: 3 ~ G.F. ~ Equipment: Blender, Juicer

Fresh and flavorful, this is the tastiest Tortilla Soup your lips will ever touch. The base is creamy with a slight sweetness and a touch of spice. The bulk ingredients soak up these delightful flavors. The soup is left uncooked so none of the vitamins or minerals are cooked out. This vibrant wholesome soup leaves one full of energy and vitality.

Ingredients

For the Broth:
8 roma tomatoes, roughly chopped
2 medjool dates, pitted
50 grams brazil nuts, soaked and strained
4 cloves garlic
1/4 red onion, chopped
3 sprigs cilantro
1/2 cup carrot juice
1 orange, juiced
1 teaspoon lemon juice
1 teaspoon lime juice
2 tablespoons olive oil
1/8 teaspoon chili flakes
1 teaspoon oregano
1/2 teaspoon garlic powder
1 teaspoon cumin
1 teaspoon salt
pinch each black pepper and chili powder

To be folded into Broth:
3 whole tomatoes, small dice
1/2 whole mangos, small dice
1/4 bunch parsley, fine chop
1/4 bunch cilantro, rough chop
1/4 of a long English cucumber, small dice
1/2 red pepper, seeded and small dice

Optional garnish:
cilantro leaves
lime wedge

Method

1. Place all broth ingredients into the blender and blend well to create a smooth base broth.
2. Fold in secondary ingredients.
3. Let the diced ingredients macerate in the base broth for 1-2 hours, refrigerated, before serving.
4. Garnish each serving with cilantro leaves and a lime wedge.

Power House
Living Foods

Power House Living Foods Co. adds a delicious, vibrant and healthy spark to Nanaimo's restaurant scene. A visit to Power House is a positive experience beginning with a warm ambiance, modern music, positive informative staff and delicious uniquely created foods. The eco-friendly design of this health food eatery includes an array of living plants, reclaimed wooden counters and tables constructed of local maple, and walls boasting the art of Frank Armich, a Vancouver Island Artist. A chalkboard wall has been provided for patrons to express their positive thoughts, in quote or idea. Beverages are placed in chalkboard glasses, noting inspiration and garnished with apple hearts, banana spears and fresh pineapple.

The raw food menu offers a great variety of fresh juices, smoothies, mylkshakes, pizzas, wraps and salads made from whole natural foods. Power House excels with treats such as granola bars, energy bars and kale chips, which are the subject of Toni's recipe. These are amazing. They are crunchy, yet melt in your mouth and have a cheesy onion flavor.

The two Power House Living Foods Co. locations have brightened Nanaimo with their great food & spirit. Kudos to Toni Jeffries for her excellent creation and for filling taste buds and bodies with bites of bliss.

A note from restaurant owner Toni Jeffries: Power House has been created to provide the freshest nutrient dense raw, vegan food to our community, while educating and empowering people to make healthy food choices, and to be aware of the effects of food choices on ourselves and our environment. We promote the consumption of fresh produce, as these foods are bursting with vitamins, minerals, phyto-nutrients and fibre. Consuming fresh fruits, vegetables, nuts and seeds in their natural state provides pure energy to fuel us throughout the day. Our menu is entirely gluten- and dairy-free, with no refined sugars or flours, additives or preservatives. Our food creations are made with your health in mind and we are passionate about serving you the very best!

THE MOST AMAZING RAW,
GLUTEN FREE DESSERTS EVER!!
- KIMBERLY

I LOVE YOU
POWER HOUSE!
- SAM & JIM

LOVED THE FOOD HERE!
- KAYLEIGH

LOVE WHAT YOU EAT,
EAT WHAT YOU LOVE!
- TRISH

UM...YUM!!
- NICOLE

Green Smoothie
Power House Living Foods

Preparation time: 10 minutes ~ Yields: 16 ounces, 1-2 servings ~ Level of difficulty: 1 ~ Equipment: Food processor or Blender ~ G/F & S/F

Green Smoothies are the best way to boost your nutrition and fill up on incredible healthy foods. This smoothie is full of fiber and protein, and is packed with nutritious greens. It flaunts the lovely flavor trio of orange, banana and pineapple. The greens show their color yet their flavor is hidden behind the sweet delicious flavors of the fruit. This smoothie tastes great and fills you up with energy and vitality.

Ingredients

2 Valencia oranges
1 medium banana
1/2 cup fresh or frozen pineapple
1 cup fresh spinach

1 cup fresh kale
4 small leaves dandelion greens
3 tablespoons hemp hearts
1 cup filtered water

Method

1. Blend all ingredients well in a food processor or blender until smooth. Enjoy!

Sour Crème & Onion Kale Chips
Power House Living Foods

In Advance: Soak the cashews for 2 hours ~ Preparation time: 25 minutes, and 12 hours to dehydrate ~ Serves: 6 ~ Level of difficulty: 2 ~ Equipment: Dehydrator, Blender ~ G/F & S/F

Power House Living Foods says these Sour Crème and Onion Kale Chips are To Live For! They taste better than regular chips and are rich in healthy protein, omegas, B12 and trace minerals. Fortunately, this healthy snack is kid and adult approved. The sour crème and onion flavor is delicious and the chips are nice and crunchy. Just like regular chips you probably can't eat just one, but you will feel good after eating these.

Ingredients

2 bunches of kale, washed with stems removed
1 1/4 cup soaked cashews, drained
1/2 cup water
1/4 cup lemon juice
1/4 cup hemp seeds

1 tablespoon coconut
1/16 teaspoon Stevia
3/4 cup nutritional yeast
1 1/2 tablespoon apple cider vinegar
1/4 cup green onion
1/4 teaspoon Himalayan crystal salt

Method

1. Place the prepared kale in a large bowl.
2. Place the remaining ingredients in the blender and blend well.
3. Pour the mixture over the kale, a little at a time, coating each piece of kale evenly by hand.
4. Place sparsely onto mesh dehydrator tray, allowing room for airflow.
5. Dehydrate for 12 hours at 114 degrees F.
6. Allow the chips to cool 20 minutes.
7. Remove gently from trays, and place in an airtight container for up to one week.

The beautiful state of California flaunts many temptations.
It produces masses of almonds, artichokes, dates, figs, kiwi fruit, olives, pistachios, prunes, raisins, clovers, strawberries and walnuts.

I love to taste sweet

California wine while eating the states fresh fruits and nuts.

California produces more agriculture than any other state.
Full of great vegan restaurants, California is, in my experience, the most vegan friendly of all the states.

I am happy to have tasted this glorious place.

Golden Gate Bridge, San Francisco

Malibu, California

Millennium Restaurant

Millennium Restaurant is a giant in the vegan scene and is considered, in some circles, the world's top high-end vegan restaurant. Millennium serves some of the most innovative and involved recipes I have discovered. The dishes marry ingredients and techniques from diverse cuisines and celebrate organic, seasonal and local ingredients.

The mastery of Millennium Restaurant's cuisine can be tasted in the recipes in Best Vegan. Included are The Chanterelle, Chive & Tofu Pot Stickers, which burst with the flavors of chanterelle mushrooms, garlic, chives and chile oil. The Red Rice and Fava Bean Salad is a five-star salad filled with fresh greens, mint, apricot and orange zest. The Roasted Kabocha Squash Salad with Sweet Chipotle Dressing and Spiced Pumpkin Seed Brittle is a bitter sweet love affair that is put together beautifully, dressed superbly and put out to impress. The Sweet Chipotle Dressing highlights the warm squash, and the brittle gives the dish a sweetness that is balanced by spicy greens. Bite by bite these dishes are bits of Millennium heaven.

When visiting Millennium Restaurant I feel as though I am emmersed in elegance and classic beauty. The Parisian-style dining room flaunts checkered tile flooring, French windows, fresh white table cloths and stunning chandelier lighting.

The restaurant hosts a variety of special annual dinners, such as the Heirloom Tomato Dinner, which is offered every August, and the Chilies and Beer Dinner held in September.

The success of Millennium Restaurant is often credited to the exceptional Chef Eric Tucker. Eric graduated from the acclaimed Natural Gourmet Institute and his education, health knowledge and experience with high-end dining inspired many of Millennium Restaurant's dishes.

An incredible chef, quality ingredients and a stunning interior make Millennium Restaurant internationally famous and locally fabulous. I look forward to spoiling myself again with taste of Millennium Restaurant's brilliance in my home and at the fantastic restaurant.

Top 10 Upscale Vegan Restaurants in America
Shape.com

The Top 8 Vegetarian Restaurants In America
PETA

5 Top Vegetartian Restaurants World Wide
Swide

Travellers' Choice 2012 Winner
Trip Advisor UK

Millenium Pot Stickers

Pot Stickers

with Chanterelle, Chive & Tofu with Black Vinegar Dipping Sauce
Millennium Restaurant

Preparation time: 50 minutes ~ Serves: 4 ~ Level of difficulty: 4

Chef Eric's notes: Look for pot sticker wrappers in Asian markets as well as many supermarkets. Chanterelles can hold their own with the garlic chives and chili oil. Chinese black vinegar is also available at Asian markets. If chanterelles are not available, substitute with oyster or maitake mushrooms. Pea greens are young and tender pea vines you may find in tangled bundles at the farmers' market. Chili oil is oil infused with crushed or whole chili peppers. If you can not find it you can make it on your own.

Ingredients

For the Pot Stickers:
1/4 pound or 2 cups Chinese chives or scallions, cut into 1/2 inch lengths
2 cups pea greens
1/2 pound sautéed chanterelles, diced
1/4 pound firm tofu, crumbled
1 teaspoon tamari
1/2 teaspoon toasted sesame oil
1 teaspoon ginger, minced
1/4 teaspoon white pepper
1 teaspoon cornstarch
salt to taste
pot sticker wrappers
1 cup water

For the Black Vinegar Dipping Sauce:
1/4 cup tamari
2-3 tablespoons black vinegar
1 teaspoon unrefined sugar (optional)
1 tablespoon scallion, thinly sliced
chili oil to taste

Method

1. Blanch the chives in a small saucepan with boiling, salted water for 1 minute. Immerse the chives in ice water, then squeeze out as much moisture as possible. Place in a mixing bowl.
2. Blanch the pea greens in boiling water for 20 seconds. Immerse the pea greens in ice water, then squeeze out as much moisture as possible. Finely chop and add to chives.
3. Mix in remaining Pot Sticker ingredients and adjust seasoning to taste.
4. Fill each pot sticker sheet with 1 heaping tablespoon of filling. Moisten the edge of the wrapper with water. Fold over the wrapper and crimp the edges.
5. Sear as many dumplings as will comfortably fit in a large sauté pan. Use a small amount of oil and sear over medium-high heat.
6. When each side of the dumplings has browned, slowly add 1 cup of water to the pan and cover for 1 minute. Remove the lid and allow the water to evaporate.
7. Remove the pot stickers from the pan.
8. Combine Black Vinegar Dipping Sauce ingredients and serve.

Asian Long Bean and Tempeh Salad

Millenium Restaurant

Preparation time: 35 minutes ~ Level of difficulty: 3 ~ Serves: 4

Millennium's Chef Eric's tip:

Tempeh really lends itself to sweet and spicy glazes as well as being seared with coconut oil, which adds a nutty quality to the tempeh. If you can get your hands on really fresh tempeh all the better. It's nuttier and usually doesn't contain vinegar, which, while tempering the mold growth, gives the tempeh a slight sour flavor. Out here in the San Francisco Bay area we will use Dragon Line Tempeh, a local artisan product, which showcases tempeh's nutty umami qualities.

Ingredients

For The Tempeh:
3 tablespoons tamari
2 tablespoons palm sugar or agave
1/2 teaspoon chile sambal or chile paste
1 tablespoon coconut oil
1 pound tempeh, cut into 1/2-inch cubes
1 tablespoon lemongrass, thinly sliced
2 teaspoons garlic, minced
1 tablespoon shredded coconut
Thai basil leaves

For the Long Bean Salad:
4 cups long beans, cut into 3- or 4-inch lengths
vegetable oil
1/4 cup shallot, thinly sliced
2 kaffir lime leaves, fine chiffonade
juice of 2 limes
salt to taste

Method

For the Tempeh:
1. Combine the tamari, sugar and chile, and reserve.
2. Heat the coconut oil over medium heat.
3. Sauté the tempeh, stirring often, for 5 minutes or until it develops a crust.
4. Add the lemongrass and sauté until it browns. Add the garlic and coconut and sauté until the coconut starts to brown.
5. Add the tamari mixture and sauté until it glazes onto the tempeh.
6. Toss with the basil leaves and set aside until ready to toss with the Long Bean Salad.

For the Asian Long Bean Salad:
1. Heat a wok or a large pan over high heat.
2. Sear the long beans in two batches, until just barely starting to wilt. Remove to a bowl.
3. Toss the long beans with the remaining ingredients.
4. Top with the glazed tempeh and serve.

Roasted Kabocha Squash Salad

with Sweet Chipotle Dressing and Spiced Pumpkin Seed Brittle
Millennium Restaurant

Preparation time: 45 minutes ~ Serves: 6 ~ Level of difficulty: 5 ~ Equipment: Blender, Baking sheet ~ G/F

This first-rate salad is put together beautifully, dressed superbly and put out to impress. It's not as simple to throw together as a chop, chop and dress salad. It is like creating a elegant salad experience at home. The warm squash is perfection when glazed in Sweet Chipotle Dressing. The dressing is one of my favorites—slightly sweet and slightly spicy. The pumpkin seed brittle is a delicious element and all the sweetness is balanced out with spicy greens. It's an extraordinary salad. Enjoy!

Chef Eric notes: Kabocha squash's slightly nutty flavor lends itself well to this dressing and glaze. Feel free to substitute with any of the squashes in the Kuri family. I prefer bitter greens to balance the sweet and spicy dressing. Chipotle chilies in adobo are available in small cans at many mainstream and Mexican grocery stores.

Ingredients

For the Sweet Chipotle Dressing:
1-2 chipotle chilies in adobo
3 tablespoons maple syrup
1 shallot, rough chopped
1/2 cup cider vinegar
1/2 cup grapeseed or light vegetable oil
1/2 cup extra virgin olive oil
salt and pepper to taste

For the Squash Wedges:
6 1/2 inch thick wedges of Kabocha or other Kuri squash
olive oil as needed
3 tablespoons maple syrup
salt and pepper to taste

For the Spiced Pumpkin Seed Brittle:
1/4 cup maple syrup
1/3 teaspoon baking soda
2/3 cup pumpkin seeds, toasted
1/4 cup agave nectar
1 teaspoon cumin seeds
1/2 teaspoon salt

For the Salad:
bitter salad greens for six, frisee, radicchio, escarole
seeds from 1 pomegranate

Method

For the Sweet Chipotle Dressing:
1. In a blender, combine all of the Sweet Chipotle Dressing ingredients except the oil and salt and pepper. Blend until smooth.
2. With the motor running, slowly add the oil to achieve a thick emulsion. Add salt and pepper to taste.

For the Squash Wedges:
1. Pre-heat oven to 350 degrees F.
2. Prepare a baking sheet with non-stick spray or parchment paper.
3. Place the squash wedges on the pan.
4. Mix the Sweet Chipotle Dressing with the maple syrup.
5. Brush the squash wedges with the dressing, and sprinkle with salt and pepper to taste.
6. Bake for 25 minutes, basting with the dressing after 10 minutes.
7. Serve slightly warm.

For the Spiced Pumpkin Seed Brittle:
1. Heat maple syrup in a skillet over medium heat until it has reduced by one third and is one shade darker.
2. Add the baking soda, stir well, and turn off the heat.
3. Add the remaining ingredients and stir until the syrup coats all of the pumpkin seeds and starts to crystallize, about 3 minutes.
4. Pour onto the prepared baking sheet.
5. Cool to room temperature before serving. Break apart into small pieces

Assembly

1. Place a Squash Wedge on the edge of a serving plate.
2. Toss the bitter salad greens with dressing to taste, and mound in the center of the plate.
3. Drizzle a little more dressing around the plate.
4. Sprinkle with Spiced Pumpkin Seed Brittle and pomegranate seeds.

Red Rice and Fava Bean Salad

with Chermoula Vinaigrette

Millennium Restaurant

Prep time 50 min ~ Level of difficulty 4 ~ Serves: 4 (with extra dressing left over) ~ S/F~G.F.~ Equitment needed: Coffee grinder

This is a healthy, tasty dish that's not simple to make, but worth the effort. The flavors are bold and combine well. The dish incorporates the bright flavors of greens, mint, apricot and orange zest. The beans and rice combine to form a complete protein and I feel satisfied and energized after eating this dish. It's a salad that works well as a meal as it has so many different components. I like to make this for a dinner party with girlfriends who appreciate delicious, healthy food with five star flavor. If I am in the mood for a less bold and lighter dish I add fresh cherry tomatoes instead of using sundried tomatoes, which have a stronger flavor.

Ingredients

For the Salad:
1 1/2 cups water
1 cup Bhutanese red rice
salt to taste
1 cup spring onions, thinly sliced
olive oil as needed
1 1/2 cup fresh fava beans, shelled, peeled and
blanched
1/3 cup sun-dried tomato, diced
1/3 cup dried apricot, diced
2 cups loosely packed watercress or arugula
leaves from 1/2 bunch of mint
1/4 cup pine nuts, toasted
orange zest
salt and pepper to taste

For the Chermoula Oil:
2 teaspoons whole cumin
1 teaspoon whole coriander
1 teaspoon whole allspice
1/3 teaspoon black cardamom seeds
1 teaspoon paprika
1/2 teaspoon dried dill
1/4 teaspoon cayenne
1/2 teaspoon salt
zest of 1 orange
1 cup grapeseed or olive oil

For the Chermoula Vinaigrette:
1/2 cup Chermoula oil
juice from 1 orange
1/4 cup sherry vinegar
salt and pepper to taste

Method

For the Chermoula Oil:
1. Grind the cumin, coriander, allspice and black cardamom seeds in a coffee grinder.
2. Place the ground spices into a small saucepan, and add the rest of the ingredients. Simmer to a slight bubbling for 10 minutes.
3. Cool to room temperature before using.

For the Chermoula Vinaigrette:
1. Combine the Chermoula oil with the rest of the Chermoula Vinaigrette ingredients. Set aside.

For the Salad:
1. Bring water to a boil in a saucepan with a tight fitting lid. Add the rice and salt. Simmer covered for 25 minutes. Remove from heat and let steam for 10 minutes.
2. Place the prepared rice on a sheet pan and cool to room temperature.
3. In a large sauté pan, sauté the spring onion in olive oil over medium heat until it is just starting to brown.
4. Add the fava beans and sauté for 1 minute.
5. Add the sun-dried tomato, apricot and 1 1/2 cups of the rice. Add 2 ounces of the Chermoula Vinaigrette. Toss and remove from heat. Adjust salt and pepper to taste.

Assembly

1. Toss the watercress or arugula and mint with 1 ounce of the Chermoula Vinaigrette.
2. Place a portion of the watercress or arugula in the center of a plate.
3. Place a portion of the fava salad atop the watercress.
4. Sprinkle with pine nuts and orange zest, and drizzle with more vinaigrette. Add salt and pepper to taste.

Some of the VeggieGrill Team

The VeggieGrill Owners

Veggie Grill

Locations

Los Angeles ~ Encino
16542 Ventura Blvd, Encino, CA ~ West Hollywood
8000 W Sunset Blvd, Los Angeles, CA ~ The Dome in Hollywood
6374-A Sunset Blvd., Hollywood, CA ~ L.A. Farmers Market
110 S Fairfax Ave, Los Angeles, CA ~ Westwood Village
10916 Lindbrook Dr, Los Angeles, CA ~ Santa Monica
2025 Wilshire Blvd, Santa Monica, CA ~ Plaza El Segundo
720 Allied Way, El Segundo, CA ~ Rolling Hills Plaza
2533 Pacific Coast Highway, Torrance, CA ~ Long Beach - The Marketplace
6451 E Pacific Coast Hwy, Long Beach, CA ~ University Center - Irvine
4213 Campus Drive, Irvine, CA ~ Irvine Spectrum Center
81 Fortune Drive, Irvine, CA ~ Irvine Crossroads
3972 Barranca Parkway Suite A, Irvine, CA ~ Plaza de la Paz in Laguna Niguel
27321 La Paz Road, Laguna Niguel, CA
Northern California ~ Santana Row
3055 Olin Ave #1030, San Jose, CA
Oregon ~ Cedar Hills Crossing
3435 SW Cedar Hills Blvd, Beaverton, OR~ Downtown Portland
508 SW Taylor Street, Portland, OR ~
Tanasbourne Village
2065 NW 185th Ave., Hillsboro, OR ~
Washington ~Downtown Seattle 1427 4th Ave, Seattle, WA
 South Lake Union 446 Terry Ave N, Seattle, WA ~University Village
2681 NE University Village Street, Seattle, WA

The VeggieGrill is a delicious fast vegan food chain that is a great success and rapidly expanding.
At Veggie Grill the bun your burger sits in is whole wheat, the burger may taste like chicken but it's made of healthier, non-genetically modified soy, rice and wheat products. Veggie Grill allows customers to be even healthier in their fast food ways. Would you like a side of fries with your meal or some steamed kale or quinoa pilaf?
The Veggie Grill is styled as a new age fast food restaurant. It's bright and comfortable, modern and casual.
The restaurant is at the start of a new trend—a wave that will keep growing. Someday this trend will become a tsunami of success and leave behind many vegan fast food restaurants. The time has come to make them the norm across North America. Traditional fast food chains better watch out. Bite by bite, veggie burger by unchicken burger, something much better is coming your way!

Vegetarian Restarant in LA"
Search

"One of LA's top 10 New Restaurants"
City Search

"One of LA's top 10 New Restaurants"
Los Angeles Times

"One of LA's "Can't-miss Cheap Eats"
Los Angeles Magazine

"Restaurant of the Year"
VegNews Magazine

"Best Fries in the OC"
Irvine World News

"Best American Restaurant"
Los Angeles Times Readers Choic
Awards

"Best New Restaurant in the OC"
OC Register - Best of Orange County

Grillin' Glaze

VeggieGrill

Preparation time: 15 minutes ~ Yields: slightly over 1 ½ cups ~ Level of difficulty: 1.5 ~ Can be G.F.

The chefs at VeggieGrill knew what they were doing when they created Grillin' Glaze. The chain is famous serving vegan food that appeals to all. This fills the restaurants with meat lovers and inspires people to turn over a vegan leaf. This recipe could be part of the secret. The liquid smoke gives food the hearty, succulent taste of a home-cooked BBQ or grilled feast, cooked to perfection. Use as a glaze on grilled, baked, fried, sautéed or stir-fried vegetables or veggie proteins. I love to slice up potatoes and mushrooms and bake them with a little bit of Grillin' Glaze, or top and fry a veggie burger to take it to a whole new level.

Ingredients

1 cup low-sodium tamari
(for G.F. use gluten free low-sodium tamari)
1 tablespoon Cholula hot sauce, or your favorite brand
1/2 teaspoon ground black pepper
1/2 tablespoon agave nectar

1/2 cup pineapple juice
2 tablespoons apricot jam
1 teaspoon liquid smoke

Method

1. Combine all ingredients in a medium-sized saucepan.
2. Heat over low heat and simmer for 10 minutes. Whisk to thoroughly combine all liquids.
3. Remove from heat. Brush or spoon glaze on while it is still hot to add flavor, color and a nice shine. Store extra in a covered container; refrigerate until ready to use.

Brownies
VeggieGrill

Preparation time: 50 minutes ~ Yields: 20 pieces ~ Level of difficulty: 3

Fudgey in the middle and cakey on the outside, this tassty chocolate brownie recipe really is the best!

Ingredients

2 cups vegan margarine
4 cups evaporated cane juice
4 teaspoons vanilla extract
8 tablespoons egg replacer
1 1/2 cups water
4 cups baking flour or all-purpose flour

1 teaspoon baking powder
1 teaspoon baking soda
2 1/2 cups cocoa powder
2 1/2 cups walnuts, chopped
1/2 teaspoon sea salt
powdered sugar for garnish

Method

1. Pre-heat oven to 350 degrees F.
2. In a sauce pan melt the vegan margarine.
3. In a large bowl combine the evaporated cane juice and vanilla. Add the melted margarine and mix well.
4. In a separate bowl whisk the egg replacer and water.
5. Add egg replacer mixture to the margarine mixture and combine well.
6. Add the remaining ingredients one item at a time, mixing well each time. The mixture will have a thick consistency.
7. Spray a 13" by 18" sheet pan with baking spray, and spread the mixture onto the pan.
8. Bake for 30 minutes.
9. Let cool, cut into 20 pieces, and sprinkle with powdered sugar.

Ravens' Restaurant

Ravens' Restaurant spoils all the senses. Inside, lovely relaxing music plays, and the restaurant is comfortable and elegant, with wood encased windows overlooking Mendocino's blue sea. The Arts and Crafts architecture and crackling fire provide a warm, welcoming ambiance. The beauty of the restaurant is a great match with its spectacular high-end vegan fare. Innovative dishes are created from culinary styles ranging from Asian and Italian to American.

The dishes' attractive presentation and exceptional flavors make Ravens' Restaurant an experience to be cherished.

Award of Excellence
Wine Spectator
Stanford Inn - Ravens' Restaurant location has been featured in *Oprah Magazine* **+ in over 139 magazines, newspapers and TV segments**

Ravens' Restaurant chef featured in
Oprah Magazine - **"The Innovative Spirit of Vegan Cooking"**

Voted one of the 3 best restaurants in Mendocino
Tripadvisor.com

"One of the very nicest things about life is the way we must regularly stop whatever it is we are doing and devote our attention to eating."

~ Luciano Pavarotti and William Wright

Chocolate Tart

Ravens' Restaurant

In Advance: Prepare dessert and chill for 2 hours ~ Preparation time: 1 hour ~ Level of difficulty 3.5 ~ Makes 1 10-inch tart ~ Serves: 8 to 12 ~ Equipment: Blender or Food processor, 10-inch tart pan, Double boiler or pot and metal bowl

Note from Ravens' Restaurant: This wonderful dessert begins with a crust of walnuts—protein with high-quality fatty acids. The chocolate ganache filling, with its silken tofu base, adds more nourishment. It's almost too good to be true—a dessert that satisfies the body as well as the palate. Create this masterpiece for a special dinner and don't tell your kids what's in it!

Ingredients

For the Chocolate Walnut Crust:
1/2 cup walnuts, toasted and chopped
1/4 cup canola oil
1/4 cup maple sugar crystals or brown sugar
1/4 teaspoon salt
1/4 teaspoon baking powder
1/4 cup cocoa powder
1 cup flour

For the Chocolate Ganache Filling:
1 1/4 pound organic silken tofu (1 plus 2/3 boxes)
1 1/4 cups water
2 vanilla beans, scraped or 1 1/2 teaspoon vanilla extract
3/4 cup evaporated cane juice or sugar
1/2 pound semisweet or bittersweet chocolate, chopped
1/4 cup sugar (use up to 1/2 a cup depending on desired sweetness)
pinch of salt

Method

Note: Start by doing the first two steps for the Chocolate Ganache Filling as it takes 45 minutes to simmer. Then pre-heat oven to 350 degrees F and start preparing the Chocolate Walnut Crust.

For the Chocolate Walnut Crust:
1. Process the walnuts in a food processor until fine.
2. While the food processor is still running, add the canola oil.
3. Scrape down the sides and add maple sugar crystals or brown sugar, salt, baking powder and cocoa. Process to combine.
4. In a large bowl, mix the walnut mixture with the flour.
5. Blend with hands until uniform in color and texture. Line the bottom of a 10-inch tart pan with parchment paper and lightly grease the sides of the pan and paper bottoms. Bake for 15 minutes.

For the Chocolate Ganache Filling:
1. Combine tofu, water, vanilla and evaporated cane juice or sugar in a large heavy-bottomed pot, breaking apart tofu with a whisk.
2. Bring to a boil, lower heat and simmer until liquid reduces and tofu turns a light golden color, approximately 45 minutes.
3. Chop the bittersweet chocolate and melt it in a double boiler. If you are not using a double boiler, boil water in a pot and put a metal bowl over the pot while water is boiling. Place chocolate inside the bowl to melt.
4. In a blender or food processor fitted with a metal blade, blend the warm tofu mixture with the melted chocolate and add 1/4 to 1/2 cup sugar (depending on desired sweetness) and pinch of salt
5. Blend until smooth and pour into pre-baked chocolate walnut crust. Chill thoroughly until firm.

Sea Palm Strudel

Ravens' Restaurant

Level of Difficulty 4 ~ Serves: 4

A note from Ravens' Restaurant: "If The Ravens' has a signature dish, the Sea Palm Strudel is it. Sea palm grows just off of the California coast, has a rich flavor, and is not slimy like some seaweed. One of the restaurant's chefs, Georgia Lane, worked with an intern, Resa Sollaway, to create this dish, originally as an appetizer. Over the years, small changes have been made. As of this writing, the following is the current version. The Sea Palm Strudel is usually served with a stir-fry of vegetables from the restaurant's garden with organic cashews, Ume Plum Sauce and Wasabi Sauce."

Ingredients

For the Filling:
4 ounces sea palm, soaked for 5 minutes in enough warm water to cover
4 cups water
6 tablespoons tamari
1 cup brown rice syrup
1 tablespoon fresh ginger, grated
1 onion, thinly sliced
2 carrots, julienned
3 tablespoons sesame oil

For the Ume Plum Sauce:
2 cups frozen raspberries
juice of 1 lime
1/4 cup Umeboshi plum puree
1 cup apple juice
2 tablespoons arrowroot

For the Wasabi Sauce:
2 1/4 teaspoons wasabi powder, mixed with enough water to form a paste
3/4 teaspoon rice vinegar
1 cup canola oil

For the Phyllo Wrapping:
1 package whole wheat phyllo dough
olive oil
black sesame seeds

Method

For the Sea Palm Strudel:
1. Preheat oven to 450 degrees F.
2. In a large saucepan, combine drained sea palm, 4 cups water, tamari and rice syrup. Over medium heat, bring mixture to a slow boil. Lower the heat and simmer until the liquid turns to syrup, about 15 minutes. Add ginger and remove the saucepan from the heat and allow to cool.
3. In a medium saucepan, sauté the onion and carrots in the sesame oil. Lower the heat and allow the onions and carrots to caramelize. Set aside to cool.

Assembly

1. Lay down one sheet of phyllo dough and brush lightly with oil. Place a second sheet on top of the first and brush with oil again. Repeat with a third layer. Sprinkle black sesame seeds over the whole third sheet. Layer two more sheets of phyllo on top of the three, brushing each with oil. Sprinkle black sesame seeds on the top layer.
2. Spread a 3-inch wide strip of the cooled sea palm mixture evenly across the bottom of the phyllo sheets, leaving 2 inches of space at the bottom. Lift the bottom edge up and over the sea palm mixture, rolling and securing the mixture.
3. Place a 3-inch wide strip of the cooled carrot and onion mixture evenly across the phyllo just above the secured sea palm mixture. Roll the sea palm up and over the carrot mixture, securing the onion carrot mixture. Continue to gently roll up. Place, seam side down, onto a greased baking sheet.
5. Bake for 15 to 20 minutes or until golden brown and heated through. Allow to rest for 5-10 minutes.

For the Ume Plum Sauce:
1. In a small sauce pan combine the raspberries, lime juice and plum puree. Cover with apple juice, using only enough to cover the mixture. Bring to a boil over medium heat.
2. Combine the arrowroot with a small amount of water, just enough to make a milky paste.
3. Carefully add the arrowroot mixture to the boiling raspberry mixture. Mix well and remove from heat.

Note: This sauce can be made ahead and refrigerated for up to 5 days. Recipe makes approximately 1 1/2 cups.

For the Wasabi Sauce:
1. Place wasabi paste and rice vinegar in a food processor fitted with a metal blade. Process until ingredients are combined.
2. Continue to process while slowly adding the oil through the feeding tube until the mixture develops into a smooth and creamy sauce.

Recipe makes approximately 1 cup.

Presentation

1. Using a serrated knife, slice the Sea Palm Strudel into 4-inch pieces. Place each piece on a plate whole, or cut each piece in half and place them on the plate with vegetable stir-fry between them.
2. Carefully pour 2 tablespoons of Ume Plum Sauce on the other side of the plate.
3. Using a squirt bottle or a pastry bag with a fine tip (you can also use a Zip-lock bag with the end cut to make a fine tip), squeeze out a thin zig-zag line of the Wasabi Sauce onto the plum sauce, so that you have many short green lines.
4. Starting at the top on the far side, drag a toothpick through the plum sauce and green lines. This will create a scalloped look. Repeat every 2 inches, switching direction each new line.

Bloodroot Restaurant

Bloodroot Restaurant is a legendary place, with a lot of personality and character. The food is absolutely exceptional. They have included many incredible recipes, which I am truly grateful for. Initially I did not want to have so many recipes from one restaurant in *Best Vegan*; yet, I could not resist. They are all so darn good!

Some of the tastiest vegan dishes come from the Bloodroot kitchen like the Mexican Mole, which is full of, un-chicken and rice and the most delicious mole sauce I have tasted. Another favorite is the Mid-eastern Lentils and Rice; this simple dish is full of onion flavors and perfectly seasoned to appease any diner.

Taking a trip to Bloodroot Restaurant is an experience of food, attitude and philosophy. When arriving, one is greeted by the friendly owners and their kitties. Owners Selma Miriam and Noel Furie explain how they choose their menu style: "We search for the real, not contrived, home cooking and street food of our neighbors around the world. Over the years we have developed recipes inspired by such diverse cultures as Mexico, Vietnam, Turkey, Jamaica and Japan, as well as many others. In addition, we want our foods to be of the season, the most delicious right now, whether from our own garden or from the farmers we have come to know as friends."

Selma and Noel have acknowledged that at Bloodroot, "Things are just different."

One is a bit more self-sufficient at Bloodroot Restaurant than at other restaurants. Visitors pay upfront and listen for their names before serving themselves. When the meal is finished, satisfied diners bus their own tables. It's a fun experience and a friendly place, and it's easy to fall into fascinating conversation with Selma and Noel or with fellow patrons. Bloodroot Restaurant is a unique and inspiring place to visit and has become a haven for East Coast activists.

So if you get to take a trip to Bloodroot Restaurant, go with an open mind and leave with a full stomach and a memorable experience.

Bloodroot........"is legendary"

New York Times

Harford Currant

Fairfield County Weekly

Bloodroot Restaurant owners, Selma and Noel

Path through the woods in Connecticut

Harvest Vegetable Platter
Bloodroot Restaurant

Preparation time: 1.5 hours ~ Serves: 8 ~ Level of difficulty: 4 ~ Equitment needed: Food processor, Blender

Warm veggies and lots of stuffing covered in amazing gravy and sweetened with cranberry sauce. Heaven! This beautiful spread is similar to classic Thanksgiving meal, but veganized and healthier. It's composed mostly of wonderfully flavored vegetables that combine beautifully in texture and flavor. I like to use kabocha squash (commonly known as Japanese pumpkin squash) for its sweet flavor. The meal leaves you feeling light and healthy, not weighed down like a classic Thanksgiving meal. Create, enjoy and entertain with love!

Notes from Bloodroot Restaurant: We don't celebrate Thanksgiving because of its questionable association with the theft of Native American land. However, we do have a harvest feast on the fourth Thursday in November as an example of how well vegetarians can eat at feasting time.

Ingredients

For the Rutabaga Potato Puree:
1 medium sized rutabaga (yellow turnip)
2 medium potatoes
1 clove garlic
2 tablespoons grapeseed oil
1/3 cup olive oil
salt and pepper

For the Roasted Parsnips and Carrots:
4 parsnips, peeled
1 medium onion
5 carrots, scraped
grapeseed oil
1/2 to 1/4 cup sunflower seeds
1/4 cup water
1 tablespoon tamari (for G.F. use gluten free tamari)
1 head of broccoli florets

For the Sweet Dumpling Squash:
4 squash
water

For the Apple Cranberry Sauce:
6 tart apples, peeled, cored and sliced
1/2 pound cranberries
1/2 cup apple juice or cider
1/4 teaspoon cinnamon
maple syrup to sweeten

For the Chestnut Stuffing:
2 cups homemade bread, slightly dry and chopped by hand or processed into bread crumbs
20 chestnuts
2 to 3 tablespoons oil
1/2 cup onion, chopped
1/4 cup shallot
2 tablespoons grapeseed oil
1/2 teaspoon dry thyme
2 tablespoons celery leaves, chopped
3 tablespoons straight leaf parsley
1 teaspoon salt
fresh ground pepper
1 teaspoon lemon juice
splash of brandy
soymilk, if needed

For the Shiitake Soy Paste Gravy:
6 shiitake mushrooms, dried
1 ancho chile pepper, dried and seeded
2 sun-dried tomatoes
1 small onion
1 to 2 garlic cloves
1/3 cup grapeseed oil
1/3 cup flour
1/2 cup nutritional yeast, optional
1 bottle of honey brown ale
1/2 teaspoon dried thyme
1/2 teaspoon dried basil
2 bay leaves
2 tablespoons tamari
1/4 cup soy paste, available at Asian markets
2 to 3 tablespoons tomato paste

Method

For the Rutabaga Potato Puree:
1. Peel the rutabaga and cut into chunks.
2. Cook for 10 minutes in boiling, salted water.
3. Add the potatoes, peeled and cut into chunks.
4. When both are cooked, drain and puree in food processor or mixer while still hot.
5. In small pot, sauté the garlic in the grapeseed oil.
6. Add to the puree together with the olive oil. Season to taste with salt and pepper.

For the Roasted Parsnips and Carrots:
1. Pre-heat the oven to 450 degrees F.
2. Place the parsnips, onion and carrots into a shallow roasting pan and moisten with a little grapeseed oil. Roast, stirring often, until browned.
3. When almost done, add the sunflower seeds.
4. When well-cooked, add the water and tamari. Cover with foil to keep warm or re-heat covered.
5. When ready to serve, steam the broccoli florets until barely done and add to the mixture.

For the Sweet Dumpling Squash:
1. Slice the squash in half lengthwise and scrape out seeds.
2. Either slice the squash crosswise in scalloped slices, or for a more elaborate dinner, stuff the squash halves with Chestnut Stuffing.
3. If simply slicing them, put them in a roasting pan, water, cover with foil and bake at 350°F until they are just soft.

For the Apple Cranberry Sauce:
1. Place the tart apple and cranberries in a pot with apple juice or cider and cinnamon.
2. Cook covered until cranberries are popped and apples are soft.
3. Add enough maple syrup to sweeten.

For the Chestnut Stuffing:

1. Cut an X into each chestnut.
2. Sauté 5 to 6 at a time in oil, stirring often, for 5 to 10 minutes. Let cool.
3. Peel. Be sure to remove inner brown skin.
4. Finely chop onion and shallots and sauté in grapeseed oil in a large pan.
5. Add bread crumbs, thyme, celery leaves, straight leaf parsley, salt, fresh ground pepper, lemon juice and brandy.
6. Slice the chestnuts into the mixture, which should be slightly moist. Add soy milk if needed.
7. Salt and pepper the insides of the squash halves and moisten with oil.
8. Heap stuffing into squash halves and place in a roasting pan.
9. Add a 1/2 inch of water to the pan, cover with foil and bake at 350 degrees F until squash are done, about 45 minutes.

For the Shiitake Soy Paste Gravy:

1. Place the shiitake mushrooms, ancho chile pepper and sun-dried tomatoes in a bowl. Cover with boiling water and set aside.
2. When shiitakes have softened, remove them from the water and squeeze out the liquid back into the bowl before thinly slicing the mushrooms.
3. Sauté shiitakes, onion and garlic in grapeseed oil. When onions just begin to caramelize, add flour and nutritional yeast, if using.
4. Use a blender to puree ancho chile, sun-dried tomatoes and reserved liquid.
5. Add to the pot with the stiitake mushroom mixture, along with water, honey brown ale, thyme, basil, bay leaves, tamari, soy paste and tomato paste.
6. Bring to a simmer and adjust the seasoning to taste. Add water as needed.

Presentation

Serve the Rutabaga Potato Puree and the Sweet Dumpling Squash with the Shiitake Soy Paste Gravy. The Roasted Parsnips and Carrots, and Apple Cranberry Sauce all make a very pretty platter.

Grilled "Chicken" Mexican Mole

With Mediano Rice & Pinto Beans

Bloodroot Restaurant

In Advance: Soak pinto beans for at least 4 hours, then cook ~ Serves: 6 to 8 ~ Level of difficulty: 4.5 ~ Preparation time: 1.5 Hours ~

Can be G.F. if use gluten free soy based chicken substitute~ Equiment: Blender or Food processor

Note from Bloodroot Restaurant: There are many different moles in Mexico, especially in Oaxaca. This is an exceptionally delicious one, adapted from a Rick Bayless recipe. Most of the Mexican food ingredients are available at Latina markets. Bloodroot Restaurant uses a faux soy-based "chicken" for this tasty recipe. Alternatively, you can use seitan or tofu.

Ingredients

For the Mole Sauce:
3 large tomatillos, quarted
3 roma tomatoes, halved lengthwise
large onion, cut into wedges
6 pasilla chillies, dried, stems removed and seeds reserved
3 cups water, boiled
1 ripe plantain, coarsely diced
1/3 cup grapeseed oil
1/3 cup peanuts
1/3 cup sesame seeds
1/3 cup raisins
2 ounces Mexican chocolate
1/2 teaspoon oregano
1/2 teaspoon cinnamon
1/2 teaspoon cloves
1 tablespoon coarse salt
1/4 cup oil
piloncillo or brown sugar to taste

For the Grilled "Chicken":
6-8 cups of soy-based chicken substitute, seitan or tofu, cut into strips (for G.F. use tofu or gluten free chicken substitute)
salt & pepper

For the "Chicken" Marinade:
3 cloves garlic, crushed
1/2 cup cider vinegar
2 tablespoons ancho chile powder
1 tablespoon dried oregano
3 tablespoons canned chipotle chili sauce, such as La Costena Chipotles in adobo
1/2 cup grapeseed oil

For the Mediano Rice and Pinto Beans:
pinto beans, soaked at least 4 hours, cooked and salted (served with dish use as many as much as desired)
2 shallots, chopped
3 cups grano mediano rice, raw
2 tomatoes, diced
corn tortillas

For Garnish:
peanuts
cilantro
avocado slices
lime wedges

Method

For the Mole Sauce:
1. Place tomatillos, roma tomatoes and onion into a roasting pan under a broiler to char. Turn to char on all sides (cook until veggies turn slightly black). Remove from broiler and turn off broiler.
2. Place pasillas in a pan under the warm but turned off broiler to soften for a minute or two. Once soft, place pasillas into a bowl and add the boiling water to soak.
3. Place the plantains into a large frying pan together with grapeseed oil and sauté.
4. Add the peanuts and sesame seeds. Stir to combine.
5. When the seeds begin to brown, add the raisins, charred vegetables and pasillas with their liquid. Add Mexican chocolate, oregano, cinnamon, cloves and coarse salt. Stir the simmering mixture until the chocolate melts.
6. Working in batches, purée the contents of the frying pan in a blender or food processor, placing each finished batch into a bowl. 7. Return unwashed pan to the stove. Heat the oil on low heat and add purée. Cook over low heat, stirring, until the mixture thickens and turns deep red.
7. Taste and adjust seasoning to taste. Add piloncillo or brown sugar to taste, if desired.

For the "Chicken" Marinade:
1. Place all ingredients into a bowl and stir to combine.
2. Salt and pepper the "chicken" strips and toss with the marinade. Refrigerate.

For the Mediano Rice and Pinto Beans:
1. Sauté shallots and mediano rice in oil until the rice is translucent.
2. Add water and simmer until almost done, then add the tomatoes.
3. Cook pinto beans seperately.

Assembly

1. When ready to serve, broil 5-6 strips of "chicken" for each diner.
2. Make a small pool of Mole Sauce on the plate. Set the crisp "chicken" strips on the Mole Sauce.
3. Warm 2 corn tortillas per plate on top of the grill or in the oven. Add Mediano Rice to the plate and the Pinto Beans.
4. Garnish with peanuts, chopped cilantro, avocado slices and lime wedges and serve the tortillas on the side.

Bloodroot Burger

Bloodroot Restaurant

Preparation time: 1 hour ~ Yields: 20 Burgers ~ Level of difficulty: 3 ~ Can be G.F ~ Equipment: Food processor

Bloodroot Restaurant Note: A combination of grains, nuts and vegetables make a delicious burger. This recipe makes a lot; we shape the burgers, place each one in plastic wrap and freeze. Then they are brushed with oil and broiled as needed.

Ingredients

1 cup quinoa, cooked
1 cup basmati rice, cooked
1 cup well-cleaned French lentils, cooked
1 cup whole almonds
1 small onion, diced
3 to 4 garlic cloves, peeled and minced
10 ounces spinach, kale or Swiss chard leaves, shredded
2 tablespoons grapeseed oil
1/2 teaspoon ground cumin
1/2 cup tamari (for G.F. use gluten free tamari)
2 teaspoons ground black pepper
2 small potatoes, washed and finely grated

Bloodroot Restaurant serves Bloodroot Burgers with:

pita bread
salad
raw onions
dill pickle
ketchup
barbecue sauce

Method

1. Combine quinoa, basmati rice and French lentils in a large bowl.
2. Toast whole almonds at 300 degrees F until well dried out (approximately 12 minutes). Remove and cool.
3. Place almonds into a food processor and chop finely. Set aside.
4. Sauté onion, garlic and greens in grapeseed oil with ground cumin.
5. When the onions turn golden and begin to brown, turn off the heat and add to the quinoa mixture.
6. In a separate bowl, combine almonds, tamari, pepper and potatoes and add to quinoa mixture. Mix thoroughly.
7. Form into patties. Wrap extras in plastic wrap and freeze.
8. When ready to serve brush each burger with grapeseed oil and broil on both sides.

Oatmeal Sunflower Bread
Bloodroot Restaurant

Yields: 2-3 loaves ~ Preparation time: 4.5 hours ~ Level of difficulty: 4 ~ Equipment: 3 small loaf tins (9"x 5"x 3") or 2 larger ones, Stand mixer, optional

What a delight it is to make bread from scratch. It's a bit of effort and a lot of fun. This bread is my favorite. It is dense but fluffy and tastes wholesome and homemade. If you serve this bread with Mushroom Walnut Pate you have made a perfect match!

Ingredients

4 cups boiling water
3 cups rolled oats
2 tablespoons yeast
2 tablespoons salt
1/4 cup grapeseed oil

1/2 cup molasses
1/4 cup sour dough starter (if available)
5 to 8 cups unbleached white flour
1/2 cup sunflower seeds
1/2 cup sesame seeds
lecithin oil to grease loaf tins

Method

1. Pour boiling water over rolled oats and let cool for 1/2 hour in a large bowl. Oatmeal must be no more than warm when yeast is added.
2. In a stand mixer or by hand add yeast to the oatmeal and stir in salt, grapeseed oil, molasses, sour dough starter (if using) and gradually add the flour.
3. Knead a good 20 minutes if working by hand and least 10 minutes in a machine. Add enough flour to make the dough silky, not tough and dry.
4. When dough seems the right texture, add the sunflower seeds and sesame seeds. Mix into bread dough thoroughly and set dough aside to rise for 1 1/2 to 2 hours, covered with a dishtowel.
5. Use lecithin oil to grease the loaf tins.
6. Once dough has risen, punch it down on a floured board and shape it into loaves. Place in the pans and let rise another 1/2 hour.
6. Pre-heat oven to 350 degrees F and bake bread for 40-45 minutes.
7. Turn the loaves out onto racks to cool.

Mushroom Walnut Pate

Bloodroot Restaurant

Yields: 2 cups ~ Preparation time: 25 minutes ~ Level of difficulty: 3 ~ G/F ~ Equipment: Coffee grinder, Food processor

A note from Bloodroot Restaurant "Our intent was to develop a recipe for a dairy-free spread for bread. The resulting pate is better flavored, we think, than the best liver pâtés. We serve it as a salad, though it could be made of softer consistency for a dip, can be frozen and defrosted with no change in consistency, and of course, is delightful spread on bread—especially rye, fresh out of the oven. The recipe which follows is tricky and somewhat time consuming. A good quality food processor is a necessity."

Ingredients

1/3 cup sunflower seeds
2 tablespoons sesame seeds
1/2 pound or 2 cups mushrooms
3 tablespoons shallots, peeled and coarsely chopped
2 tablespoons grapeseed oil
salt and freshly ground pepper to season
1/2 cup walnuts
1 small clove garlic, peeled
1/2 teaspoon dried oregano
1/2 teaspoon dried tarragon
1/3 cup olive oil

1/3 cup grapeseed oil
2 tablespoons lemon juice
1/4 pound tofu
2/3 teaspoon prepared mustard
1 1/2 to 2 tablespoons tamari (for G.F. use glu

Serving suggestion: Portion into a 1/2 inch thick green pepper ring on a bed of Boston lettuce with cucumber slices and celery hearts. Sprinkle with paprika and top with fluted raw mushrooms.

Method

1. In a small coffee grinder, pulverize the sunflower seeds and sesame seeds until very finely ground. Turn seeds into a bowl and set aside.
2. In a food processor, coarsely cut the mushrooms. Add the shallots, and chop finely.
3. Place the mixture into a clean dish towel or piece of cheese cloth and twist the towel slowly over a small bowl to extract the juice. Reserve this liquid.
3. Heat the grapeseed oil in a frying pan and when hot, add the mixture and sauté over high heat, stirring, until it is browned and separated. Season with salt and freshly ground pepper and set aside.
4. Place the ground seeds into the unwashed food processor and add walnuts, garlic, oregano and tarragon.
5. Turn processor on and very slowly begin to add the grapeseed and olive oils until the mixture becomes a very stiff paste.
6. Alternately add lemon juice and pieces of tofu, and the oil as machine runs, stretching the oil addition to take about 10 minutes. If the mixture becomes so stiff as to turn machine off, then pate is proceeding properly. Add a little lemon juice to start it up again.
7. Add the prepared mustard and tamari and continue to process. If the pate seems too stiff add a little of the reserved mushroom juice or water. If oil was added too quickly, you may find signs of separation as machine works. If this happens, turn the processor off, pour the excess oil back into a measuring cup and restart the processor. After a minute or two, begin dribbling oil in again until it is properly incorporated.
8. In a bowl, fold together the mushroom mixture and the contents of the food processor. Chill.

Mid-East Lentils and Rice

Bloodroot Restaurant

Preparation time: 45 minutes ~ Serves: 6 ~ Level of difficulty: 3 ~ S/F ~ Can be G/F if not served with pita bread

This recipe is simple and inexpensive yet tastes incredible. Its just so darn good! Everything about it comes together perfectly. The flavors of olive oil and sautéed onions give the dish rich flavor.

Ingredients

2 cups French lentils, raw
1 cup long grain white rice
2 large Spanish onions
1 cup olive oil
1 1/2 teaspoons salt

1 teaspoon paprika
1/2 teaspoon cayenne

Bloodroot restaurant serves this recipe with green bean stew, olive and walnut accompaniment and pita bread.

Method

1. Pick over French lentils to remove stones and debris. Place into a soup pot with 3 1/2 cups water and bring to a boil. Turn heat down and simmer 15 minutes.
2. Add the long grain white rice and 1 cup of water and simmer for 15 minutes.
3. Meanwhile, thinly slice the Spanish onions. In a frying pan, sauté the onions in olive oil until golden brown.
4. Add the onions and oil into the pot of lentils and rice. Add salt, paprika and cayenne. Continue cooking until lentils and rice are well-cooked. Adjust seasoning to taste.

Vietnamese Summer Rolls

with Peanut Sauce
Bloodroot Restaurant

Preparation time: 1 hour 20 minutes ~ Serves: 6-8 ~ Level of difficulty: 4 ~ G/F

These summer rolls are fresh and light and full of flavor. When one is dipped into the incredible peanut sauce, eaters find, they never want to go back to a regular summer roll!

Ingredients

For the Summer Rolls:
3/4 pound fresh tofu
2 to 3 tablespoons grape seed oil
1 large or 2 small carrots, shredded
1 cup red cabbage, shredded
1 cup celery hearts, diced
1 teaspoon toasted sesame oil*
4 ounces mung bean vermicelli*
2 tablespoons basil (preferably Thai), chopped
2 tablespoons cilantro
1/4 cup mint leaves
1 cup peanuts, roasted
Vietnamese rice paper "spring roll" rounds.* Six inch diameter (3 per diner) or 9 inch diameter (1 to 2 per diner).
1 lettuce leaf per roll
peanuts, sesame seeds and mint leaves to taste

For the Peanut Sauce:
1 teaspoon lemongrass,* chopped very fine
1 tablespoon tamarind concentrate*
2 tablespoons lime juice
2/3 cup organic peanut butter
1 cup coconut milk
1 teaspoon agave nectar
2 teaspoons salt
1 shallot or scallion, minced

Serve garnished with mung bean sprouts, cucumber spears, slices of red onion and a half teaspoon of chili paste with garlic*

Available in Asian markets

Method

For the Summer Rolls:
1. Cut the tofu into 1/2 inch slices. Wrap it in absorbent paper and place it on a plate in the refrigerator with a can or container on top to weight and compress it for one hour.
2. Dice the drained and compressed tofu. On medium-high heat, fry the tofu cubes in grapeseed oil, stirring often, for up to 10 minutes, or until the cubes are golden. Remove and place in a bowl.
3. Add carrot, cabbage and celery to the pan and stirfry briefly over medium heat. Remove and add to tofu bowl. Sprinkle mixture with toasted sesame oil.
4. Bring a small pot of water to a boil and add the mung bean vermicelli. Cook just a few minutes, until tender. Drain and slice coarsely.
5. Add the vermicelli, basil, cilantro and mint leaves to the tofu mixture.
6. Season this mixture to taste with rice wine vinegar, Kim Lan soy paste* or soy sauce. Refrigerate, covered.

For the Peanut Sauce:
1. Place lemongrass in a bowl. Add tamarind concentrate and lime juice, stirring to combine.
2. Gradually add peanut butter and thin with coconut milk.
3. Add agave nectar, salt and shallot or scallion. Adjust seasoning for a salty, sweet and sour flavor. Refrigerate.

Assembly

1. Soak one spring roll round at a time in a bowl of hot tap water. Place onto a damp dish towel.
2. Lay a flat lettuce leaf onto each rice paper. Top with filling, peanuts, sesame seeds and mint leaves. Fold the bottom up, then sides in, and roll as tightly as possible. Place on serving plate with garnish or cover with plastic wrap and refrigerate until ready to serve.

Marinated Tofu Salad

Bloodroot Restaurant

Preparation time: 25 minutes ~ Serves: 4-6 ~ Level of difficulty: 2 ~ G/F

The dressing is tasty, the vegetables fresh and flavorful and the tofu nicely marinated. This salad is easy to prepare and tastes great.

Ingredients

For the Marinated Tofu:
1 cup grapeseed oil
1/4 cup Chinese toasted sesame oil
2 tablespoons lemon juice
1/4 cup tamari
2 tablespoons rice wine vinegar
1 1/2 pounds firm tofu

For the Salad:
1 head Chinese napa cabbage, shredded
Center salad with:
carrots, shredded (as much as desired)
scallion, chopped (as much as desired)
daikon, shredded (as much as desired)
gomahsio (sesame seed condiment found in Asian markets) (as much as desired)

Method

For the Marinated Tofu:
1. Whisk together the grapeseed oil, Chinese toasted sesame oil, lemon juice, tamari and rice wine vinegar.
2. Cut the tofu in half horizontally, then diagonally, to make thin triangles 1/2 to 1/4 inch thick. Lay in a shallow container and desired amount of the marinade reserve extra. Cover and chill.

For the Salad:
1. Arrange the Napa cabbage on the plates.
2. Top with tofu triangles.
3. Place carrots, scallions and daikon in the center.
4. Dress with marinade and top with gomahsio.

Coconut Oil Pie Crust

Bloodroot Restaurant

Preparation time: 1 hour ~ Serves: 8 ~ Level of difficulty: 3 ~ S/F

A note from Bloodroot Restaurant: This crust is the easiest of any to make, and the hardest to work with. It is more difficult in hot, humid weather. This recipe has been adapted from a lard version.

Ingredients

1 cup all-purpose flour
½ teaspoon salt
½ teaspoon ground cardamom (optional)
2 tablespoons sugar
scant ⅓ cup coconut oil
2 tablespoons water

Method

1. In a small bowl combine flour and salt. Add the cardamom, if using, and the sugar. Stir together with a dry whisk.
2. Liquefy the coconut oil on low heat.
3. Add water to the coconut oil and use a fork to stir. Immediately dump liquids into the flour mixture and continue to stir with fork. It will quickly form a very sticky ball.
3. Place the pastry ball between 2 sheets of plastic wrap or wax paper. With a rolling pin, roll out a shape as close as possible to a circle.
4. When rolled, slide the plastic-wrapped dough onto a rimless cookie sheet.
5. Carefully remove the top piece of plastic wrap and discard. Invert a 9 inch Pyrex pie plate over the pastry, and carefully turn it all right side up. As you cautiously remove the second piece of plastic wrap, edge the crust into the pan. Use your floured fingers to shape the edge.
6. Prick the bottom with a fork and sprinkle lightly with flour.
7. Refrigerate until cold, 5 to 10 minutes. Bake for 10 minutes weighted with foil and beans at 375 degrees F.
8. Remove the foil and add fruit or other filling, or complete baking (about 15 to 20 minutes) and fill pie shell afterwards.

Chocolate Silk Pie Filling or Pudding

Bloodroot Restaurant

Preparation time: 20 minutes ~ Serves: 8 ~ Level of difficulty: 2

Sweet, creamy, silky chocolate comfort food. Serve as a pie filling with your favorite crust or as a pudding in individual glass bowls or custard cups. Enjoy!

Ingredients

1 (14 ounce) can coconut milk
2 cups almond milk
scant 1/2 cup sugar
4 ounces bittersweet chocolate
1/3 cup cornstarch
2 tablespoons unsweetened cocoa powder

1 tablespoon instant coffee powder
1/2 teaspoon salt.
2 teaspoons vanilla extract

Serve with slivered toasted almonds and coconut milk to pour over the top

Method

1. Combine the coconut milk, almond milk, sugar, chocolate, cornstarch, cocoa powder, instant coffee and salt in a medium-sized pot.
2. Whisk the ingredients together over medium heat. Cook, stirring frequently, until mixture comes to a visible simmer and has thickened, 10 minutes. Remove from heat.
3. Add the vanilla extract and stir well. Turn into individual custard cups, a pie shell or into a large glass bowl.
4. Serve with slivered toasted almonds and coconut milk poured over the top.

Macerated Summer Fruit Tart

Bloodroot Restaurant

In Advance: Prepare and refridgerate for several hours ~ Preparation time: 20 minutes if making tart 40 minutes ~ Serves: 8 ~ Level of difficulty: 3

Sweet and fresh, this Macerated Fruit can be a made into a fruit tart or eaten alone for a simple treat.

Ingredients

1 lime
3 tablespoons Demerara sugar or brown sugar
1/2 teaspoon salt
1/2 teaspoon ground cardamom
1 tablespoon gin
1 pound of fruit: strawberries quartered lengthwise,
whole blueberries, whole raspberries, pitted cherries,
peaches, sliced.

Coconut Oil Pie Crust (recipe page 68) or other
prepared crust
2 tablespoons cornstarch

Optional: serve with vegan ice cream, cake or soy yogurt

Method

1. In a bowl, combine the juice and grated rind of the lime, Demerara sugar or brown sugar, salt, ground cardamom and gin. Stir to combine.
2. Add fruit. Refrigerate several hours or up to 1 1/2 weeks.
3. Place fruit into a strainer set over a bowl. Let drain for 30 minutes.
4. Prepare the tart crust. Let cool.
5. Add the cornstarch to the drained fruit juices and bring to a simmer on low heat, stirring constantly until the liquid is clear and had thickened. Adjust sugar to taste.
6. Add the drained fruit to the crust. Pour juices over pie.
7. Don't cut until the juices have set up.

The sunlight, blue skies and glorious beaches make

Florida an incredible place to enjoy life. Sweet fruits hang from farmers' branches offering juicy oranges, plump peaches and an array of tropical fruit.

Surrounded by thousands of small islands, the Sunshine State relaxes with its beaches and laid back attitude then impresses and excites with the flashiness of cities like Miami.

"In this life we cannot do great things. We can do small things with great love."

~ Mother Theresa

Karma Cream

Soft and creamy, dense and flavorful, rich and sweet, Karma Cream is lick by lick delightful. The undeniable treat talents of this ice cream shop led me to its special inclusion in Best Vegan. This is not a vegan restaurant, but it has the best vegan treats.

Karma Cream is a cute little shop that is known for excellent vegan and dairy ice cream, coffee drinks and sweet baked treats. Made with coconut cream base and sweetened with agave the shop's vegan ice cream is thick and sweet and, for many, preferable to dairy ice cream.

Karma Cream serves heaps of tempting options like the decadent triple chocolate, delicious lemon cookie and sweet maple walnut. The house-made waffle cones are sweet and crunchy and toppings like the dairy-free whip cream, chocolate espresso fudge and all-natural ricemallow fluff help make Karma Cream the best ice cream experience around.

Finalists for The Best
Vegan Ice Cream in America
~PETA

Five Thumbs Up!
~ gainesvilleeatsbetter.com

Chocolate Chip Cookies

Karma Cream

In Advance: Make the dough and refrigerate for 36 hours ~ Preparation time: 35 minutes ~ Yields: One dozen ~ Level of difficulty: 2.5 ~ Equipment: Stand mixer

Sweet, perfect, delicious chocolate chip cookies. These are the ultimate comfort food. Adults love them and they are very kid-friendly! They are fun to make and a delight to eat.

Ingredients

5 cups organic, unbleached all-purpose flour
1/2 teaspoon fine sea salt
2 teaspoons aluminum-free baking soda
2 cups Earth Balance, or other vegan margarine
2 1/2 cups organic pure cane sugar

1 tablespoon unsulphured molasses
1 tablespoon organic double fold pure vanilla extract
1/4 - 1/2 cup water
1 1/2 cups organic and Fair Trade semi-sweet chocolate chips

Method

1. In a medium bowl, mix together flour, salt and baking soda, set aside.
2. Place Earth Balance in the mixing bowl of the stand mixer. With paddle attachment, beat at medium speed until smooth.
3. Increase to high speed and gradually cream together Earth Balance and cane sugar. Beat until mixture is light and very fluffy. Stop when necessary to scrape down sides of bowl.
4. Shut off mixer to add molasses and vanilla and mix until nearly incorporated.
5. Set speed to low and gradually add flour mixture. Add water mid-way through and mix until incorporated.
6. When flour is well incorporated add chocolate chips. You may mix the dough by hand to ensure even distribution.
7. Wrap dough tightly in plastic wrap to prevent exposure to air. Refrigerate for 36 hours.
8. Pre-heat oven to 350 degrees F.
9. Scoop out dough one quarter cup at a time. Shape into tight balls, and press into half-inch thick, even circles.
10. Bake cookies on the oven's center rack until the cookies are slightly golden, about 10-15 minutes.
11. Remove cookies from oven. Let them cool for 3 minutes, then transfer to cooling rack and cool completely. For slightly crispier cookies, allow to cool completely on the baking pan.

Ice Cream Sandwiches

Karma Cream

Preparation time: 30 minutes, 2 hours to refrigerate dough ~ Yields: 14 cookies ~ Level of difficulty: 2.5 ~ Equipment: Stand mixer

These are sweet, tempting, little devils (or maybe they are chocolaty angels?) Regardless, they are delicious! I smoosh a big pile of Rice Dream ice cream in the middle, which brings me to the conclusion that I have created a little bit of heaven. These are fairly easy to make and even easier to eat.

Ingredients

2 3/4 cups organic, all-purpose flour
1/2 cup organic and fair trade cocoa powder
2 1/2 teaspoons aluminum-free baking powder
1/4 teaspoon fine sea salt

3/4 cup Earth Balance or other vegan margarine
1 1/2 teaspoons organic double fold pure vanilla extract
1 1/2 cups organic pure cane sugar
1-2 tablespoons organic soy milk or almond milk

Method

1. In a medium bowl, soft together flour, cocoa powder, baking powder and salt. Set aside.
2. In the stand mixer, using the paddle attachment, cream together Earth Balance and sugar at high speed until fluffy.
3. Add vanilla and incorporate.
4. Reduce speed to low and gradually mix in half of the flour mixture.
5. Add the soy or almond milk, mix thoroughly and add the remainder of the flour mixture. Continue mixing until a thick dough is formed, adding more milk if needed.
6. Wrap dough tightly in plastic wrap and refrigerate for at least 2 hours.
7. Roll dough onto a non-stick surface and roll out to 1/4 or 1/8-inch thick.
8. Cut into the desired shape, ensuring there is an even number of cookies.
9. Place cookies two inches apart on a baking sheet lined with parchment paper. Using a fork, poke holes in the cookie using an even pattern that covers the entire cookie.
10. Bake on the oven's middle rack at 350 degrees F for 10 to 15 minutes or until firm.
11. Remove from the oven and allow to cool on the pan. For softer cookies, allow to cool on the pan for 3 minutes, then transfer to a cooling rack.

Assembly

1. Place one cookie upside down on a plate.
2. Add one or two scoops of your favorite vegan ice cream on the cookie, and press down gently with a spoon or spatula.
3. Place a second cookie, right side up, on top and gently press together.

Optional

Place the same mold used to shape the cookies onto a parchment paper-lined baking sheet. Press softened vegan ice cream into the mold. Gently remove by pressing down on the ice cream and lifting the mold. Make half as many ice cream molds as cookies. Store in the freezer until the cookies are ready. When cookies are completely cool, sandwich pre-molded ice cream between two cookies and enjoy.

Atlanta, Georgia

Cafe Sunflower

Café Sunflower is an exceptional veggie restaurant. In its two decades of operation it has been nationally recognized with numerous awards. Currently there are two locations in Atlanta, Georgia, both of which are cozy and relaxing. The Buckhead location has an earth-toned dining room, which is warmly lit in the evening by orange globes and the Sandy Springs location is housed in a large, impressive building as shown on the adjacent page.

The restaurant serves a blend of Asian, Caribbean, Mediterranean and classic American cuisine and is well known as the place to get a great vegan meal in Atlanta.

Popular meals include the Sesame 'Chicken', which is full of flavor and bursting with fresh veggies and brown rice. The Southern Polenta Napoleon is another favorite, which includes grilled coconut cornmeal cake layered with mock ham, veggies, portabella mushroom and artichokes.

The wonderful flavor combination demonstrates creativity gone well. At the end of a meal a server showcases incredible desserts so you can't help but want one. My favorite is the Carrot Cake. It's truly the best I have tasted and the restaurant has brilliantly included the recipe in Best Vegan so you can enjoy this sweet moist cake yourself!

Honorable Mentions

Atlanta Magazine
The Best of Atlanta
Best Place to Take a Vegetarian

Buckhead Guidebook
recommends Cafe Sunflower

Citysearch.com
2001 Audience Winner
Best Vegetarian Food

Atlanta Magazine ~ Readers Choice
The Sunday Paper ~ Readers Choice
Where The Locals Eat
Creative Loafing
Best of Atlanta ~ Readers Pick
Best Vegetarian

City Voter
Atlanta Hotlist

Carrot Cake

Cafe Sunflower

Preparation time: 45-50 minutes ~ Serves: 10 to 15, makes two cakes ~ Level of difficulty: 3 ~ Equipment: Stand up mixer, Two 9-inch round cake pans

This is the best carrot cake I have tried, and it's an absolute winner. It's exceptionally moist, perfectly sweetened and full of carrots, raisins and nuts. The carrot cake is famous at Café Sunflower and keeps many guests coming back for more. Try out the recipe for yourself and become a talented carrot cake creator!

Ingredients

For the Cake:
3 cups unbleached flour
2 teaspoons baking powder
2 teaspoons baking soda
2 teaspoons cinnamon
1/2 teaspoon nutmeg
1 teaspoon sea salt
3/4 cup oil
2 cups sugar (see Tip)
1/2 cup vanilla soy milk
1/2 cup water
2 cups carrots, grated
1 cup walnuts, chopped
1/2 cup raisins

Tip: 1 1/4 cups maple syrup may be substituted for 2 cups sugar. Simply cut back the soy milk by 1/4 cup and the oil by 1/4cup.

For the Frosting:
2 1/2 cups confectioner's sugar
3 sticks of soy margarine
1 teaspoon vanilla extract
2 tablespoons soy milk

Method

For the Cake:
1. Preheat oven to 350 degrees F and grease two 9-inch round cake pans.
2. Sift the flour, baking powder, baking soda, cinnamon, nutmeg and salt together in a large bowl. Set aside.
3. In a large bowl, mix oil, sugar, soy milk and water.
4. Pour the wet ingredients into the dry ingredients and mix.
5. Add carrots, walnuts and raisins to the mixture. Stir until well incorporated.
6. Pour the mixture into round pans.
7. Bake approximately 25 to 30 minutes.
8. Cool completely before icing.

For the Frosting:
1. Blend all ingredients in a stand up mixer on low speed for one minute and then on medium speed for 3 minutes.
2. Set aside and frost carrot cake once it has cooled.

Spaghetti Squash Cakes

with Caper Soy Mayonnaise Sauce
Café Sunflower

Preparation time: 50 minutes ~ Serves: 6-7 with 12-15 cakes ~ Level of difficulty: 3

These are delicious! They are great to serve to a vegan-fearful group because they are quite similar to fishcakes and the caper sauce takes them to the next level. They're a little chewy and a little crunchy and a lot delicious.

Ingredients

For the Caper Soy Mayonnaise Sauce:
1/2 cup soy mayonnaise
1 tablespoon capers
1 teaspoon maple syrup
1 teaspoon lemon juice

For the Spaghetti Squash Cakes:
1 spaghetti squash
2 tablespoons oil
1 leek, washed and finely chopped
1 small onion, finely chopped
3/4 cup dried yellow corn grits
1/2 can coconut milk (about 3/4 cup)
1 teaspoon coriander
1 teaspoon ginger powder
1 teaspoon turmeric
1 teaspoon salt
1 1/2 teaspoons seaweed flakes
1 1/2 to 2 cups flour

Method

For the Caper Soy Mayonnaise Sauce:
1. Blend all ingredients. Set aside.

For the Spaghetti Squash Cakes:
1. Cut the squash in half and remove the seeds. Boil the spaghetti squash with the skin on for about 20 minutes or until soft enough to pull the skin off easily. Set aside.
2. Sauté the leek and onions in oil until translucent. Set aside.
3. Mix all remaining ingredients except the flour in a large bowl.
4. Add the flour gradually and stir well until the mixture resembles a thick pancake batter.
5. Using a large ice cream scoop, spoon the batter into a pan or grill warmed on medium-high heat. When the cake bottoms are firm, turn them over and press them into round pancakes.
6. Serve hot with Caper Soy Mayonnaise.

Lov'n It Live

Lov'n It Live is a small cozy restaurant that serves excellent raw vegan food. Its has a wholesome attitude as it was opened to provide patrons with food for body, mind and soul.

The restaurant is located ten minutes from the busy city of Atlanta, Georgia. The atmosphere is warm and friendly and I adore how the small restaurant offers classical music, displays lovely artwork, has chess games and at times hosts live music or poetry events.

Lov'n It Live serves mains with a global influence, sweet raw treats and fresh juices and smoothies from lunch to dinner. It serves an exceptional Raw Stuffed Avocado and I am pleased the restaurant owners included the recipe in Best Vegan. It's a very popular appetizer at the restaurant, and contains ripe avocado filled with flavorful nutmeat and topped with a chunky tomato based pico topping.. Lov'n It Live also contributed a Raw Kale Salad recipe, which is simple to make and bursting with fresh garlic, onion and herb flavors. This is true soul food, raw style, for your mind body and soul... I am Lov'n It Live!

"Let Food Be Your Medicine,
Let Medicine Be Your Food."

Hippocrates

Raw Stuffed Avocado

with Pico Sauce

Lov'n It Live

In Advance: Soak almonds for 9 hours ~ Preparation time: 30 minutes ~ Serves: 4-8 ~ Level of difficulty: 3 ~ Equipment: Food processor or Blender ~ G/F & S/F

This appetizer combines wonderful flavor and creamy and crunchy textures. The dense, flavorful nutmeat is perfect and well complemented by the light, fresh Pico Sauce that goes wonderfully on top of the avocado. It's simple to prepare and vibrantly healthy. Bon Appetite!

Ingredients

4 Haas avocados, halved with pits removed

For the Nutmeat:
1 cup raw almonds, soaked
2 tablespoons onion, chopped
1/2 celery stalk
1/2 tablespoon lemon juice
pinch of cayenne
sea salt to taste (start with a large pinch)
3/4 teaspoon turmeric, more to taste
1/2 tablespoon dried organic sweet leaf basil
1/2 tablespoon dried oregano leaf
1/2 garlic clove

1 1/2 to 3 pieces sun-dried tomato, halved and soaked for 10 minutes (save water)
1 tablespoons olive oil

For the Pico Sauce:
1 onion, chopped medium fine
1/2 red pepper, chopped medium fine
2 roma tomatoes, medium chopped
2 tablespoon cilantro, or to taste
juice of 2 lemons
2 teaspoons olive oil
salt to taste
mixed greens to garnish

Method

For the Nutmeat:
1. Blend nutmeat ingredients together until the almonds are crumbly.
3. Slowly add 1/4 to 1/2 cup of water to thoroughly mix and achieve desired consistency.

Pico Sauce Directions:
1. Mix ingredients together in bowl. Set aside.

Assembly

1. Cut avocadoes in half length-wise. Sprinkle each piece with salt and pepper to taste. Place on a plate prepared with mixed greens for garnish.
2. Add approximately one ounce of nutmeat to the center of each avocado.
3. Top with Pico Sauce.

Raw Kale Salad
Lov'n It Live

Preparation time: 15 minutes ~ Serves: 4 ~ Level of difficulty: 2 ~ G/F ~ S/F

This recipe is healthy, easy to make and easy to take! This filling salad remains light and is blasted with lots of flavor and nutrition. The onions and garlic are fresh and bold, and nicely accented by the herbs, avocado and red pepper.

Ingredients

1 pound green curly kale, coarsely chopped, or local mixed greens
1 red bell pepper, thinly sliced
1 onion, chopped or thinly sliced
juice of 1/2 lemon

2 teaspoons olive oil
1 heaping tablespoon dried sweet basil leaf
1 heaping tablespoon dried organic oregano
1-2 Haas avocadoes, peeled and chopped
1-2 garlic cloves minced
salt to taste

Method

1. Place kale, red peppers, onion, lemon juice, olive oil, garlic and herbs in a bowl for mixing.
2. Peel and chop avocado and place in bowl, mixing in 1/2 at a time.
3. Add salt to taste.
4. Massage and toss ingredients. To massage kale, take bunches of kale in both hands and rub them together and repeat. You'll notice the leaves will darken, shrink in size and become silky in texture as you are doing this.

Michigan Lake Shore, Chicago

Karyn's On Green, Chicago

Karyn's On Green

There is a glamourus feeling to the low lit lounge at Karyn's on Green. The chandeliers above the sleek 22-seat bar, the classy lounge upstairs and the waterfall wall by the door all set the tone for an exceptional dining experience. The restaurant's tag line is, "making vegan sexy," and the environment says it all. The food is even sexier. Exceptionally tasty and beautifully presented, the menu features classic American dishes reinterpreted with plant-based representations of chicken, fish, chorizo and more, covering cuisine styles from Italian to Asian to raw food. The drink menu is creative and well accomplished with some faboulous cocktails like the Fair Trade Cosmo and Skinny Vegan. Karyn's knack for food, drink and business shine through her mini empire, which can be tasted at Karyn's on Green, Karyn's Fresh Corner, Karyn's Cooked, the Karyn's at Home meal-planning program and Karyn's Inner Beauty Center. Karyn motivates herself and those who come to her wanting a healthier lifestyle by asking:

"If you don't take care for your body where are you going to live?"

honorable mentions

Restaurant owner Karyn has appeared on *"The Oprah Winfrey Show"* as well as in numerous national commercials and print ads and on an album cover.

Karyn Calabrese was awarded the *First Annual Raw and Living Foods Golden Branch Award.*

Caramelized Brussels Sprouts

with Mustard Vinaigrette
Karyn's On Green

Preparation time: 25 minutes ~ Serves: 2-4 ~ Level of difficulty: 3 ~ G/F & S/F

Brussels sprouts are very good for you. They are full of vitamins, potassium and calcium and with this Mustard Vinaigrette they taste very good as well! The vinaigrette is thick and creamy with a nice mustard flavor.

Ingredients

For the Brussels Sprouts:
1 pound blanched Brussels sprouts, halved or quartered
olive oil for sautéeing
salt to taste

For the Mustard Vinaigrette:
1 shallot, minced
2 sprigs of tarragon, chopped
1/4 cup champagne vinegar or white wine vinegar
1 cup whole grain mustard
lemon juice and salt to taste

Method
1. Whisk all Mustard Vinaigrette ingredients together. The mixture can be thinned out with water if desired.
2. Blanch the Brussels sprouts in salted, boiling water until al dente, which means medium cooked, but not soft.
3. Briefly shock the Brussels sprouts in a bowl of ice water. Drain and pat dry with paper towels.
4. Sear the Brussels sprouts in a hot sautée pan on medium heat with olive oil until well caramelized.
5. Fold in as much of the Mustard Vinaigrette as desired. You should have some remaining. Season with salt to taste.

Butternut Squash Soup

with Chickpeas

Karyn's On Green

Preparation time: 1 hour 15 minutes ~ Serves: 4-8 ~ Level of difficulty: 3 ~ Equipment: Blender, Fine mesh strainer ~ Optional equipment: Deep fryer ~ G/F & S/F

Butternut Squash Soup is creamy, warm, goodness! This recipe is simple to make and very satisfying. The chickpeas on top are pan-fried and nicely seasoned. The soup is thick and creamy, a little sweet and simply delicious. Nothing's better than hot soup on a cold winter day and this one takes the cake... I mean soup!

Ingredients

For the Soup Base:
2 whole butternut squash (about 5 pounds in total)
2 14 ounce cans coconut milk
water to thin
salt
to taste
paprika for garnish

For the Chickpeas:
1/4 cup canned chickpeas, strained
1/2 teaspoon paprika
oil for frying
salt to taste

Method

For the Soup Base:
1. Pre-heat oven to 350 degrees F.
2. Cut the ends off of the squash, and discard. Cut the squash in half length-wise and de-seed.
3. Place halved squash skin side up on prepared baking sheets. Roast in the oven for about an hour or until the largest squash is soft throughout. Cool to room temperature.
4. Remove the skin and cut the squash into large chunks.
5. Combine the coconut milk with the squash in a large sauce pot and simmer, stirring occasionally until the mixture is heated throughout.
6. Remove from heat and blend the mixture on high until it is smooth and reaches the desired consistency. Add water to thin if necessary. Season with salt to taste and strain through fine mesh strainer.
7. Pour about 1 cup into a soup bowl and garnish with a sprinkle of paprika and chickpeas.

For the Chickpeas:
1. Fry the chickpeas in a deepfryer or sauce pot with oil heated to 325 degrees F until they begin to brown in color.
2. Strain the excess oil and toss with paprika and salt in mixing bowl.

Health Tip: Butternut squash contains many anti-oxidants and vitamins, and is low calorie with warming and grounding elements.

View of Boston and Cambridge,
Massachusetts

Becon Hill Boston, Massachusetts

Massachusetts Park

Life Alive

Warm wraps, soups, salads, hot meals, cold smoothies and great prices. Classic American health food all meat-free and as good as it gets. Life Alive uses all organic produce and makes meals that leave you feeling great. The restaurant has created a fabulous reputation, a dash of fame and a loyal clientele that has kept Life Alive growing and expanding.

Life Alive splashes the restaurant walls and décor with bright color, serves vibrant food and hires energetic staff. Vibrancy, joy, flavor and health is at a whole new level at Life Alive!

Best Vegetarian!
Boston's Best 2012

"Flavor Lust in Cambridge"
PETA Prime

The Sufi Poet
Balsamic Vinaigrette Salad with Red Lentil Hummus
Life Alive

In advance: Prepare Balsamic Vinaigrette and Red Lentil Hummus ~ Preparation time: 10 minutes ~ Level of difficulty: 2 ~ Serves: 2-4 ~ S/F & G/F

Fresh and bright, The Sufi Poet salad is the perfect mix of sweet, savory and healthy ingredients. Energizing and tasty it makes an excellent lunch or side plate.

Ingredients

2 ounces of organic spring mix
1/2 cup carrots
sprinkling of quartered cucumbers (cut into quarters length wise then chopped)

sprinkling of apple pieces
1 tablespoon unsweetened dried cranberries
1 tablespoon raw cashews
Red Lentil Hummus (see page 101)
Balsamic Vinaigrette (see page 102)

Method

1. In a large bowl, combine all ingredients except Balsamic Vinaigrette and Red Lentil Hummus.
2. Mix desired amount of Balsamic Vinaigrette into salad.
3. Divide salad into individual portions and scoop 1-3 spoonfuls of Red Lentil Hummus on each bowl of salad.

Red Lentil Hummus

Life Alive

Preparation time: 40 minutes ~ Serves 6 ~ Level of difficulty: 2 ~ Equipment: Fine mesh strainer, Food processor, Rice Cooker ~ G/F & S/F

This is a particularly tasty Red Lentil Hummus recipe. It is blasted with fresh garlic flavours. Enjoy!

Ingredients

1.5 cups of organic red lentils
4 tablespoons of Bragg liquid aminos
1 teaspoon black pepper
1 tablespoon organic, cold pressed extra
virgin olive oil
1/2 oz crushed organic raw garlic

Method

1. Puree mixture with a high velocity food processor until light and fluffy.

Balsamic Vinaigrette

by Jamie Isabella Parker

Preparation time 10 minutes ~ Serves: 4 ~ Level of difficulty 1.5 ~ G/F & S/F

This is a fantastic recipe. Enjoy!

Ingredients

1 tablespoon dijon mustard
1 teaspoon light brown sugar
1-2 small garlic cloves, minced
1/2 teaspoon salt

1/4 teaspoon black pepper, ground
2 tablespoons balsamic vinegar
1 tablespoon red wine vinegar, optional
1/4 cup extra virgin olive oil

Method

1. Mix all ingredients except oil together.
2. Add oil to mixture and mix well with whisk.

Organic Garden Café

The Organic Garden Café has been serving delicious food that is organic, vegetarian and mostly raw since 1999.

The food is tasty and energizing like the recipes included for the Beanless Hummus and Raw Hummus Wrap. The restaurant's menu offers breakfast, lunch, dinner and delicious desserts. The drink menu includes beer and wine along with healthy shots like the Ginger Shot and fun smoothies like the Chai Frappe, a creamy, cold, sweet chai.

The restaurant has an inviting ambiance that is warm and casual. There is a scattering of tables outside and the inside is nicely decorated with creations from local artists.

Health is a priority here, as the owner, Robert, spent years studying natural health. Through his studies, he concluded that an organic vegan and raw diet gave the body ideal nutrition and support to excel. His passion for health and helping others led him to open the Organic Garden Café.

The restaurant has clearly been a great success that continues to grow and thrive. The combination of delicious food, great intentions and noble practices bodes well for the Organic Garden Café to have a long and abundant life!

Bons Award
Best of North Shore

Best of Boston
Boston Magazine

One of two Best Vegetarian Restaurants
The Boston Phoenix

Dining Out "Top Picks For 2003"
The Boston Globe

What lies behind us and what lies before us are small matters compared to what lies within us.

~ Ralph Waldo Emerson

Raw Beanless Hummus

Organic Garden Café

Preparation time: 15 minutes ~ Yields: 4 cups ~ Level of difficulty: 2 ~ Equipment: Food processor ~ G/F & S/F

This raw humus is similar to regular humus—creamy and delicious. It's fairly simple to make and full of fresh ingredients that are healthy and flavorful. This humus is perfect in a Raw Nori Wrap, which is one of my favorite raw foods—it's light, nutritious and bursting with flavor. Begin with half the salt required in this recipe, and add more to taste. Enjoy!

Ingredients

2 cups zucchini, peeled and cut into 1/2 inch pieces
1/2 cup tahini
1 cup hulled sesame seed, ground
1/4 cup lemon juice

1 tablespoon fresh garlic cloves, chopped
1 teaspoon sea salt
3/4 teaspoon cumin powder

Method

1. Blend all ingredients together in a food processor until creamy.

Raw Nori Wrap

Organic Garden Café

Preparation time: 10 minutes ~ Serves: 2-4 ~ Level of difficulty: 2 ~ G/F & S/F

Since venturing into vegan-hood I have been a huge fan of Raw Nori Wraps. These wraps are particularly tasty because of the delicious raw hummus inside them. Nori is a type of seaweed found in Asian markets, health food stores or regular grocery stores.

Ingredients

2 cups Raw Beanless Hummus (see page 105)
4 sheets of Nori
greens of choice, such as romaine lettuce or baby spinach

1 cup each bell pepper, avocado and tomato
1/2 cup cucumber, cut into long, thin strips

Method

1. Spread 3 1/2 tablespoons of hummus on each piece of Nori.
2. Add a small handful of greens.
3. Lay the bell pepper, avocado, tomato and cucumber lengthwise on top of the greens.
4. Roll the Nori sheet and wet the end with a dressing, water or tamari to seal it.

Veggie Galaxy is considered by some the best vegetarian restaurant in Boston, which one can see from the regular line-up of fans waiting to get in. The restaurant is eye-catching from the outside: it has a spaceship look with wide windows, a shiny metal door and bright green neon sign. Inside has a more classic diner look, scattered with tables, a long bar and red bar stools.

From breakfast to dinner, Veggie Galaxy serves exceptionally tasty and meatless diner-style food.

Creativity shines through on the menu with dishes like the Seitan Loaf, which tastes

like classic meat loaf you can make for yourself with the included recipe. Veggie Galaxy is also known for desserts like the creamy, chocolately Taza Cheesecake. Veggie Galaxy is continually exceptional and is a Boston treasure!

"Best Vegetarian Restaurant"
The Boston Phoenix

"Best Vegetarian Restaurant"
The Weekly Dig

"Best Vegetarian Restaurant"
Boston Magazine

Taza Chocolate Cheesecake
Veggie Galaxy

Preparation time: 45 minutes ~ Bake time: 1.5 hours ~ Makes 1 10-inch cake ~ Level of difficulty: 4 ~ Equipment: 10-inch circular springform pan, Hand held electric mixer

Dense, rich, chocolate filling with a creamy sweetness that melts in your mouth. It's enough to make your taste buds wild. That it is a non-dairy cheesecake is undetectable by the seasoned dessert indulger. This recipe will leave you with some extra cheesecake batter, which you can enjoy by the spoonful!

Ingredients

For the Graham Cracker Crust:
3 cups graham cracker crumbs
1/2 cup + 2 tablespoons cane sugar
3/4 cup + 2 tablespoons Earth Balance or other vegan margarine

For the Taza Chocolate Cheesecake Batter:
1 1/2 pounds Toffuti Better Than Cream Cheese or other vegan cream cheese
1 1/4 cups cane sugar
1/4 cup cornstarch
1 1/4 teaspoon salt
1 tablespoon + 1 teaspoon vanilla extract
1 cup + 3 tablespoons coconut milk
3 cups Taza chocolate (60%), or other vegan chocolate, chopped

Note: Veggie Galazy is proud to use Taza Chocolate for this recipe. If it is not available in your area, another brand of vegan cholocate can be substitued, although it may affect the texture or cook time.

Method

For the Graham Cracker Crust:

1. Place graham cracker crumbs and sugar into a bowl and mix thoroughly to combine.
2. Melt Earth Balance and pour into graham cracker crumb mixture. Stir to incorporate.
3. Grease a 10-inch springform pan with Earth Balance or a vegan non-stick spray.
4. Pour graham cracker crumb mixture into the springform pan. Press firmly to pack crust mixture onto the bottom and up the sides. Set aside.

For the Taza Chocolate Cheesecake Batter:

1. Measure cane sugar, cornstarch and salt into a small bowl and mix thoroughly to combine, making sure there are no lumps of cornstarch.
2. Place vegan cream cheese into a mixing bowl and mix on medium speed until smooth.
3. With the mixer still running, slowly add sugar/cornstarch mixture.
4. Mix for another minute or so, stopping to thoroughly scrape the bowl and paddle or beaters.
5. Increase the mixer speed to medium-high speed and slowly drizzle in vanilla extract, continuing to mix until light and fluffy, about 4-5 minutes.
6. Measure coconut milk into a saucepan and bring to a boil. Remove from heat and add chopped chocolate, stirring until completely melted, smooth and lump-free.
7. With mixer running, pour melted chocolate/coconut milk into cream cheese mixture.
8. Mix for 2 minutes then stop mixer and thoroughly scrape bowl. Mix for an additional 2 minutes, then transfer batter into the graham cracker crust.

Seitan Loaf

with Chipotle Balsamic Glaze
Veggie Galaxy

Preparation time: 45 minutes ~ Yeilds: 2 small loaves ~ Level of difficulty: 3.5 ~ Equipment: Food processor

This dish reminds me of going home to eat at my dad's and step-mama's place... after they went vegetarian. It has all the classic meat loaf flavors, and is homey, comforting and traditional, yet meat-free. Serve with mashed potatoes or sautéed Swiss chard for delightful comfort food that is a pleasure to prepare.

Helpful Hint: The Chipotle Balsamic Glaze is delicious, yet has a very strong flavor so use it... but don't over use it.

Ingredients

For the Seitan Loaf:
canola oil for cooking
2 medium carrots, peeled, small diced
4 stalks celery, small diced
Spanish onion, peeled and small diced
2 cloves garlic, minced
salt and pepper to taste
2 pounds house-made seitan (or your favorite store bought variety)
1/2 cup ketchup
1/4 cups mustard
1 tablespoon vegan Worcestershire sauce

1 tablespoon agave syrup
1 bunch scallions, thinly sliced
1 tablespoon pureed chipotle
1 cup Panko bread crumbs
1 tablespoon oregano, chopped
1 tablespoon rosemary, chopped
2 tablespoon tamari
2 teaspoon crushed black pepper

For the Balsamic Chipotle Glaze:
1 cup good quality Balsamic vinegar
1 tablespoon ketchup
1 tablespoon pureed chipotle

Method

For the Seitan Loaf:
1. Pre-heat oven to 350 degrees F.
2. Heat a pan over medium-high heat for 2 minutes. Add a coating of canola oil, and sauteé the carrot, celery and onion for 3-4 minutes, turning frequently.
3. Add garlic, season with salt and pepper, and sautée for 1 minute more, until the garlic is gently cooked. Transfer to large bowl and set aside.
4. In a food processor, mince seitan until it becomes completely crumbled. Add the seitan to the prepared vegetables.
5. Add all remaining ingredients, combining with your hands until consistently mixed.
6. Divide the mixture in half, and shape each half into a small loaf.
7. Bake loaves for 15-20 minutes on a sheet pan lined with parchment paper.

For the Chipotle Balsamic Glaze:
1. Combine all glaze ingredients in a small sauce pan. Simmer until the mixture is reduced by half.
2. Remove from heat, and serve over a bed of your favorite mashed potatoes and sautéed Swiss chard. Coat seitan loaves and drizzle the plate with Chipotle Balsamic Glaze.

608 Congress St Portland, ME

Green Elephant Vegetarian Bistro

A note from Green Elephant: "Green Elephant provides innovative, delicious and healthy Asian-inspired fare for any palate, vegan or otherwise.

Dan's mother, who owned a restaurant in Thailand, taught him how to cook from a very early age. Each morning, he would wake up and be put to task peeling garlic, chopping onions, making curry paste and executing other tedious preparations. His mother never used written recipes, and by cooking alongside her he began to develop his own personal style.

Dan brought this style to vegetarian cuisine with flavorful success. Green Elephant has been featured in *Maine* magazine, *Maine Food & Lifestyle* magazine and has won the *Portland Phoenix* Reader's Choice award for "Best Vegetarian" many years running.

Green Elephant has formed a strong, passionate team of chefs and staff over the years. Delicious vegetarian food coupled with an energetic atmosphere makes Green Elephant an important destination place for carnivores and vegetarians alike."

Portland, Maine Head Lighthouse

"The future belongs to those who believe in the beauty of their dreams."

~ Eleanor Roosevelt

Chocolate Orange Mousse Pie

Green Elephant Vegetarian Bistro

Preparation time: 20 minutes ~ Serves: 8 ~ Level of difficulty: 2 ~ Equipment: Food processor, Double boiler or pot and metal bowl

On a scale from one to ten, this dessert is an 11. Creamy chocolate with a hint of orange bitter and a crunch of graham chocolate work together impeccably. It seems unjust that a dessert so wonderful is lighter than most and so simple to make. We'll just keep that our little secret!

Ingredients

1 12 ounce package of silken tofu
2 tablespoons orange liqueur, optional
1/2 cup coconut milk
12 ounces semi-sweet vegan chocolate chips
1 pre-made vegan chocolate graham cracker crust
sliced and toasted almonds and grated orange peel
for garnish

Method

1. Blend tofu, orange liquor and coconut milk in a food processor until just smooth.
2. Melt the chocolate in the double boiler or bring a small pot of water to a boil and place the chocolate chips in a medium sized metal bowl over the boiling water. Stir the chocolate constantly as it melts.
3. Put the melted chocolate into the food processor and mix with the tofu mixture until creamy.
4. Pour into the prepared chocolate graham cracker crust. Chill in the refrigerator.
5. Top with sliced almonds and orange peel for garnish and serve.

Fried Brussels Sprouts

& Wild Mushroom
Green Elephant Vegetarian Bistro

Cook time: 20 minutes if deep frying; 35-40 if baking ~ Serves: 4 ~ Level of difficulty: 2.5 ~ G/F

This dish will knock the socks off your guests next Thanksgiving dinner. It consist of tasty fried Brussels sprouts with lovely wild mushrooms and perfect flavoring.

Chef's Tip: If you don't like to deep-fry your Brussels sprouts, simply bake them in the oven by brushing them with extra virgin olive oil and tamari. Pour them on a sheet pan and roast for 35 to 40 minutes at 400 degrees F until crisp on the outside and tender on the inside. Shake the pan from time to time to brown the sprouts evenly.

Ingredients

canola oil for deep frying
1 pound Brussels sprouts, trimmed and cut in half
1 tablespoon extra virgin olive oil
3/4 cup wild mushroom such as trumpet or cremini, sliced

1 tablespoon tamari (can buy gluten free)
1/2 tablespoon Maine maple syrup, or another high quality maple syrup
sea salt and pepper to taste

Method

1. Pour oil into a medium pot 3 inches deep. Heat the oil to 350 degrees F.
2. Deep fry the Brussels sprouts, for about 3 minutes until very dark brown, almost charred, but not burned. Stir occasionally.
3. Remove the Brussels sprouts from the pot with a skimmer and place directly in a bowl.
4. Heat olive oil in heavy large skillet over high heat. Add the mushrooms and sautée until they are brown and just tender, about 5 minutes.
5. Mix in the prepared Brussels sprouts. Add tamari, Maine maple syrup, sea salt and ground pepper to taste. Stir well and then transfer mixture to plates. Serve warm.

Great Sage

Great Sage has a warm and romantic atmosphere and exceptional, creative, vegan cuisine. The restaurant is charming with brightly painted walls and modern décor that hints of Asian influence. The Great Sage menu offers cuisine styles with a variety of global influences that are made all vegan, mostly cooked with some raw food options. Each Great Sage bite is skillful, creative, vegan heaven as you can taste for yourself with the flavorful Raw Curried Samosas and delicious Tempeh Bourguignon included here.

"As a recent convert from vegetarian to vegan, I was worried about being able to go out to eat. Not only does Great Sage make it possible, Great Sage makes eating vegan a pleasure. In fact, Great Sage has become a first choice for a few of my meat eating friends as well."
Michael Wenthold

"I love that my vegan family can come here and eat with my non-vegan extended family and we all find something we love!"
An Norr

" I am a meat & potatoes guy and I look forward to dinners & breakfasts at your restaurant. Everything I've had has been filling & savory, and I've never asked, "Where's the beef?"
Craig Levin

"As a lifelong vegetarian, it has been beautiful to watch the Washington/Baltimore area become more vegetarian friendly with each and every passing year. This is the sort of place that my omnivorous boyfriend loves taking me to, because it comes second to none. For a classy night out, Great Sage is definitely the place to go!"
Aini Momaiya

"Starting this new journey of veganism, I found in Great Sage my new best friend. I can look at the menu without prejudice or worries. I am free to choose and indulge. I don't have to be deprived; I am home."
Grace Elysa Piazza Ortiz

Tempeh Bourguignon
Great Sage

This is the quintessential fall or winter meal, making one feel warm and cozy inside. It takes time to make but is well worth it. The dish resembles a classic Beef Bourguignon—when eating it, I feel as though I am indulging in a glamorous stew with the perfect combination of wine, mushrooms, vegetables and tempeh.

Ingredients

For the Mushroom Glaze:
1/4 of a yellow onion
1/4 of a carrot
3 celery stalks
2 cups mushroom stems
4 cups vegetable stock
3/4 bottle syrah wine
1 tablespoon salt
1 teaspoon pepper
1 tablespoon porcini mushroom powder
2 tablespoons corn starch

For the Braised Tempeh:
3/4 cup syrah wine
2 tablespoons garlic, roasted

1/4 cup rice bran oil
1 teaspoon ground cardamom
1 tablespoon espresso or strong black coffee
1/2 teaspoon pepper
12 ounces tempeh

For the Vegetables:
1 carrot
1 parsnip
3/4 cup crimini mushrooms
3/4 cup portabella mushrooms
1/2 cup frozen peas
1 teaspoon white truffle oil

Method

For the Mushroom Glaze:
1. Chunk the vegetables and put them in a pot with the mushroom stems and stock. Bring to a boil and reduce to a slow simmer. Let simmer for at least 2 hours.
2. Reduce the wine from 3/4 cup to about 1 tablespoon by cooking it in a pot at medium to low temperature.
3. After the vegetables and stock have simmered, strain and discard the stems and vegetables and return the liquid to a simmer.
4. Add the wine reduction, spices and seasonings.
5. Wisk the corn starch with one tablespoon of water and add to the stock. This should thicken up nicely and have a strong mushroom/wine flavor. If the stock remains too thin, add more cornstarch/water mixture.

For the Braised Tempeh:
1. Blend the wine with the remaining ingredients, except the tempeh. Cut the tempeh into 1/2 inch cubes.
2. Toss all together including vegetables and mushroom glaze and bake covered at 350 degrees F for 40 minutes.
3. Serve.

Raw Curried Samosas

Great Sage

In Advance: Dehydrate samosa wrapper 4 to 8 hours ~ Preparation time: 35 minutes ~ Serves: 2-4 ~ Level of difficulty: 3.5 ~ Equipment: Dehydrator, Food processor ~ G/F & S/F

Raw food is so flavorful and energizing. These Raw Curried Samosas taste wonderful and leave you feeling great. The samosa wrapper is packed with curry and lemon flavors, and the stuffing is a beautiful complement. The dips are all lovely, bright and tasty. My favorite is the Chimmichurri—it is blasted with cilantro and lime flavors that are refreshing and perfect. Good job, Great Sage!

Ingredients

For the Samosa Wrapper:
1 large or two medium zucchini
1/2 tablespoon lemon juice
1/2 tablespoon olive oil
1/2 teaspoon curry powder
2 tablespoons flax seed, ground
1/4 teaspoon salt

For the Samosa Filling:
1/4 cauliflower head, cleaned
1/2 cup peas
1/2 tablespoon lemon juice
2 tablespoons cilantro
1/4 teaspoon garam masala
1/2 teaspoon salt
1 teaspoon jalapeño, diced

For the Chimmichurri Dipping Sauce:
1 bunch cilantro
1 1/2 teaspoons lime juice
3 sprigs of mint
4 tablespoons olive oil
1/2 teaspoon salt
1/4 teaspoon garlic

For the Minted Pear Puree Dipping Sauce:
1/2 of a pear
3 tablespoons water
1 sprig of mint
1/2 teaspoon agave

Tomato and Cucumber Coulis Dipping Sauce:
1/4 of a cucumber
1/4 of a tomato
1 1/2 tablespoons olive oil
1/4 teaspoon salt

Method

For the Samosa Wrapper:
1. Grate the zucchini into thin strands. Take half of the grated zucchini and blend with the rest of the ingredients.
2. Mix with the remaining zucchini and spread out on dehydrator drying rack to make a sheet. Dehydrate for 4 to 8 hours. The sheets should be dry, yet very pliable.
3. Cut the sheets into 2 inch by 4 inch rectangles.

For the Samosa Filling:
1. Pulse cauliflower in a food processor until it has the consistency of quinoa. Empty into a mixing bowl.
2. Puree the peas with the lemon juice to form a smooth paste. *Helpful Hint: A coffee grinder can work well for blending peas into a smooth paste.*
3. Mix the cauliflower, peas and remaining ingredients. Taste and adjust seasoning as desired.
4. Lay out the samosa wrappers and place about a tablespoon of filling onto each rectangle. Make triangle folds until the samosa is closed. A small amount of water may be needed to seal them shut.

For the Dipping Sauces:
1. Simply blend or process all of the ingredients and serve.

"Your work is to discover your work and then with all your heart to give yourself to it."

- Buddha

Detroit, Michigan

Inn Season Café

Inn Season Café lies just steps away from the area's Main St chaos. It has held a great and busy history here for
decades as the premier vegetarian restaurant in Michigan. Locally famed Chef Thomas has, for 25 years, been helping to create and perfect the
restaurant's menu. Inn Season Café demonstrates that a restaurant, just like a fine wine, does get better with age.
Inn Season Café explains,"While serving the vegetarian and vegan community, our hope is that everyone will enjoy our world-class flavors."
The top-notch ingredients and recipes help to create some of the best salads, stir-fries, pizzas and veggie burgers around!
Inn Season Café is genuine in its effort to give customers the most delicious and healthy cuisine possible. The success of these efforts can be seen
inside the busy restaurant, which often has a line-up of people down the sidewalk waiting to get in.

*"We believe good food is intrinsically healthy
and meant to be hearty and satisfying. "*

Inn Season Café

Delicious Distinctions:

Best of Detroit, Vegan/Vegetarian Menu --
Hour Magazine 2009/2011/2012/2013

*Among six nationwide independent restaurants with an
innovative healthy menu.*
Health Magazine

*Golden Bun Award - Best Vegetarian Food Entrées in North
America* PETA

*Golden Bun Award- North Americas Best Hometown
Veggie Burgers*
PETA

Citysearch rated it 9.2/10

Real food for real people --
Metro Access Magazine

Swedish Vegetable Cakes
Inn Season Café

Preparation time: 55 minutes ~ Serves: 4~ Level of difficulty: 4 ~ G/F

If you like the strong flavor of root vegetables you will love Swedish Vegetable Cakes. They pack a lot of flavor punch and are grounding and warming, making them a wonderful winter dish. Chef Thomas Lasher recommends highly recommend creating the sweet, creamy Mustard Sauce to go with them for the perfect flavor combination. The recipe yields more Mustard Sauce than required for one batch of Swedish Vegetable Cakes, but it keeps well and works as an excellent sandwich spread or dip.

Ingredients

For the Swedish Vegetable Cakes:
2 cups each rutabaga, carrot and parsnip, blanched then grated
1 1/2 cup onion, diced
2 tablespoons caraway seed, toasted and ground
3/4 cup bean flour (chickpea flour)
1/2 cup dried parsley
1/2 cup scallion, diced
1-2 tablespoon extra virgin olive oil
salt and white pepper to taste
steamed kale

For the Mustard Sauce:
2 cups Vegenaise or other non-dairy mayonnaise
1/2 cup whole grain mustard
1/4 cup maple syrup
salt to taste

Method

For the Swedish Vegetable Cakes:
1. Blanch rutabaga, carrot and parsnip in boiling water until just soft.
2. Place in an ice water bath to cool, then grate.
3. Sauté onion in olive oil until well done, about 5 to 10 minutes.
4. Place onion, rutabaga, carrot, parsnip and remaining ingredients in a bowl. Form into patties and cook in olive oil on a flat top grill or in a cast iron pan.
5. Serve with steamed kale and Mustard Sauce.

For the Mustard Sauce:
1. Whisk all ingredients together. Serve with Swedish Vegetable Cakes.

Braised Tofu with Quinoa
Inn Season Café

Preparation time: 30 minutes ~ Serves: 2-3 ~ Level of difficulty: 2.5 ~ G/F

This is a healthy dish that's packed with protein and has a nice, light flavor. It makes a simple, wholesome meal that's tasty and satisfying.

Ingredients

extra virgin olive oil to coat pan
2 cups cooked quinoa (about 2/3 of a cup uncooked quinoa yields 2 cups cooked)
1 block extra firm tofu, sliced into 12 triangles
1/2 cup shallots, sliced
2 tablespoons mirin (found in ethnic markets and grocery stores) or sweet rice wine

1/2 cup soup stock or water
2 tablespoons tamari
1/2 tablespoon mustard
1 tablespoon lemon juice
12 asparagus spears, or other seasonal vegetable
8 basil leaves, chopped
fresh parsley to taste
fresh chives to garnish, chopped

Method

1. Prepare quinoa. While it is cooking, work through the rest of the recipe.
2. Heat olive oil on medium heat in 10-12 inch sauté pan and add sliced tofu. Brown tofu on both sides.
3. Add shallots and continue to cook on medium heat for 3 to 5 minutes until shallots begin to brown.
4. Add mirin or sweet rice wine, stock or water, tamari, mustard and lemon juice.
5. Bring to boil, then lower heat to simmer until the liquid reduces by half. Add the asparagus, basil and parsley, simmering 3 to 4 minutes until the asparagus is just tender.
6. Serve in a bowl over quinoa and garnish with fresh chopped chives.

"One cannot think well, love well, sleep well, if one has not dined well."

Virginia Woolf

Eden Alley

"*Divine flavor for the conscious eater.*"

- Eden Alley Motto

Eden Alley ...

is a taste of heaven! It is fittingly located in the lower level of Unity Temple on
the Plaza. Here the walls are adorned in fine art by local artists and the tables are hand-painted
by a variety of artists as well. The large single room is spacious and colorful. I am uplifted by the bright art
work, lovely location and positive messages.

The most wonderful thing about Eden Alley is the food. I am a fan of its many tasty yet very healthy options, like the
create your own salad option where you can choose from dozens of items to make your perfect mix. Eden Ally also features classic comfort foods like meat loaves and burgers—take out the meat, but leave in the comfort.

Try the Spinach Mushroom Loaf that they included in this book.

Honorable Mentions

One of the Best Restaurants in America
Local Eats

Best Vegetarian Restaurant
The Pitch

Best Vegetarian Restaurant
Local Eats

The Best Breakfast in KC
from JENN

Kansas City, Missouri

Spinach Mushroom Loaf

with Tomato Basil Coulee
Eden Alley

Preparation time: 25 min ~ Cook time: 50 min ~ Serves: 6-8 ~ Level of difficulty: 3

This loaf combines the flavors and textures of loaf and stuffing. What a wonderful thing! It is chewy and soft and packed with spinach, mushrooms and wonderful herbs. The Tomato Basil Coulee goes over it perfectly. I like things saucy so I often top it with Eden Alley's Smokey Aioli Sauce as well. Superb!

Ingredients

For the Loaf:
1 large yellow onion, diced
1 1/2 tablespoons olive oil
1 1/2 tablespoons garlic, minced
1 1/2 teaspoons oregano
1 1/2 teaspoons thyme
1 teaspoon kosher salt
1 teaspoon black pepper

1/4 teaspoon chili flakes
1/2 pound fresh spinach, cleaned and de-stemmed
2 cups organic brown rice, cooked and cold
3 cups whole wheat bread crumbs
1/2 pound tofu, shredded
1/2 pound mushrooms, sautéed
Eden Alley's Tomato Basil Coulee

Method
1. Preheat oven to 350 degrees F.
2. Prepare a baking sheet with non-stick spray.
3. Place the spinach in a large mixing bowl and set aside.
4. Sauté the yellow onion, olive oil, garlic, oregano, thyme, salt, pepper and chilli flakes in a saucepan on medium heat until the onions are translucent.
5. Remove from the heat and pour the mixture onto the spinach immediately to slightly wilt the spinach.
6. Add the rice, bread crumbs, shredded tofu and sautéed mushrooms and mix well with hands.
7. Form into a loaf, making sure it is even in length, height and width. Place the loaf on the prepared baking sheet.
8. Bake for 50 minutes.
9. Let the loaf cool for at least 20 minutes to set.
10. Top with Tomato Basil Coulee (recipe on page 134.)

Tomato Basil Coulee

Preparation time: 20 minutes ~ Cook time: 30 minutes ~ Yields: 4 cups ~ Level of difficulty: 2 ~ G/F ~ S/F

Eden Alley uses this sauce in so many ways, calling it several things, but always calling it delicious. It's great for pasta, topping the Spinach Mushroom Loaf or over roasted vegetables. For the ultimate in health benefits and flavor, use local tomatoes in the peak of their season—mid to late summer.

Ingredients

1 1/2 tablespoons sunflower oil
1 1/2 tablespoons olive oil
1 medium sized yellow onion, diced
1 1/2 tablespoons garlic, chopped
1 tablespoon organic granulated sugar

1 teaspoon kosher or sea salt
1/2 teaspoon black pepper
a pinch of chili flakes
2 14 ounce cans of diced tomatoes
1 tablespoon fresh basil, chopped

Method

1. Add the sunflower and olive oils to a large stock pot, and begin sautéing the yellow onion, garlic, sugar, sea salt, pepper and chilli flakes on medium heat until the onions are translucent.
2. Add the diced tomatoes and stir well.
3. Reduce the heat and allow the sauce to simmer on low for a 1/2 hour, stirring every 10 minutes.
4. Remove the sauce from the heat and add 1 tablespoon of fresh chopped basil. Stir well.

Smokey Tomato Aioli

Eden Alley

In Advance: Prepare roasted garlic, requires 2 cups of Tomato Basil Coulee ~ Preparation time: 5 minutes ~ Yields: 2 cups ~ Level of difficulty: 1 ~ Equipment: Immersion blender or Food proc

I love sauces, but they tend to be calorie laden. I always felt like it was a bad habit, until Smokey Aioli Sauce came to my rescue. This lower calorie sauce has the most wonderful flavor and creamy texture. Using a little liquid smoke is a must! It is gives any vegan dish a hearty flavor.

Ingredients

1 1/2 cups Tomato Basil Coulee, cold (recipe on page 134)
3 tablespoons Vegenaise, or other vegan mayonnaise
2 tablespoons garlic, roasted
1/4 teaspoon black pepper
1/8 teaspoon kosher or sea salt
pinch of chili flakes
1/16 teaspoon liquid smoke

Method

1. In a deep mixing bowl, blend all of the ingredients with an immersion blender or food processor.

Health tip: Tomatoes are an excellent source of a powerful phytochemical called lycopene, which has been found to protect the body against cancer and heart disease. Tomato Basil Coulee is high in lycopene because cooked tomatoes contain more of it than raw tomatoes.

Roasted Garlic

by Jamie Isabella Parker

Preparation time: 5 minutes ~ Cook time: 30-35 minutes ~ Level of difficulty: 1 ~ G/F & S/F

Use this recipe for the Roasted Garlic needed in Eden Alley's Smoky Tomato Aioli (page 135) or Grasslands' Celery Root Crème Sauce (page 167). Roasted garlic is also great over French bread, with pasta or eaten on its own.

Ingredients

garlic bulbs (as many as you want to roast)
1-2 teaspoons olive oil per garlic bulb

Method

1. Preheat oven to 400 degrees F.
2. Peel away the outer layers of the garlic bulb skin and leaving the skin closest to the cloves intact. Using a knife, cut off 1/4 to 1/2 inch of the top of the garlic bulbs, exposing the individual cloves.
3. Place the prepared garlic bulbs in a baking pan. Drizzle 1-2 teaspoons of olive oil over each bulb, using your fingers to make sure the garlic is well coated. Cover the pan with aluminum foil. Bake for 30-35 minutes, or until the cloves feel soft when pressed.

New Brunswick is Canada's only officially bilingual province. Being a costal province it has breath-taking scenery and has been nicknamed the Picture Province. In New Brunswick, locals experience each season to its fullest with hot summers, golden leaf falls, cold snowy winters and blossoming springs.

East Quoddy Lighthouse, New Brunswick

Calactus

Snuggled away in the city of Moncton, New Brunswick, Calactus restaurant serves craveable, healthy and homey vegan food with classics from around the globe.

Calactus is an exceptional restaurant and would thrive in any large East Coast city, yet it has a casual charm that suits Moncton. The owners have captured the keys to restaurant success: great food, generous portions and good prices.

The restaurant is housed in a large, brown, home-style building that announces itself with a bright Calactus sign. Inside feels very Canadian—it is brightly painted, comfortable and earthy, boasting wooden tables, lots of plants and generous patio seating.

Calactus has given us the opportunity to make some of its comforting, wholesome food at home. The Fricot Soup recipe is one of my favorites because it is light yet full of healthy veggies and lentils. The Vegan Bolognese Sauce recipe is wonderful and hearty as well.

At Calactus I adore the global cuisine and comfort foods like the Taj Mahal Thali (Indian Curry), Enchiladas, and Lasagna. Not everything in the restaurant is vegan but it all can be. Vegetarian items can be made vegan by request—for instance, the chef will replace dairy cheese with a delicious house-made tofu crème.

For Moncton's vegan and vegetarian skeptics, Calactus gives a wonderful example of how delicious this food can be. Many meat eaters find themselves returning to the restaurant time and time again. I presume this lovely place has converted several of those meat eaters into vegans and vegetarians after they showed them how tasty this diet could be.

honorable mentions

"Where to eat in Canada"
Top rated restaurant on *Trip Advisor*
#1 in Moncton "Best use of local ingredients"
2013 Readers Choice Award

Le Fricot

Calactus

Preparation time: 35 minutes ~ Serves: 10 ~ Level of difficulty: 2 ~ G/F & S/F

Le Fricot is an Acadian soup, traditionally made with chicken, but made into delicious vegan goodness with red lentils in this recipe. The broth is creamy as the red lentils lose their form when cooked, and the vegetables and seasoning come together to make a perfectly flavored soup. It is inexpensive to make so it helps me save money and keep a light, healthy diet. I recommend making a big batch of it and freezing some so you always have a convenient, tasty meal on hand.

Tip: When buying red lentils, be sure to get split red lentils that are bright orange in color. Labeled as split red lentils or simply as red lentils, this variety will lose its form when cooked, giving the soup a creamy consistency.

Ingredients

1 large Spanish onion, small chopped
4 medium carrots, small chopped
4 cups potatoes, chopped
1 1/2 tablespoons summer savory or fresh thyme

1/2 teaspoon of pepper
1 3/4 tablespoons of salt
4 cups red lentils, washed
8 cups water

Method

1. In a large pot simmer the Spanish onion, carrots and potatoes in enough water to cover the vegetables.
2. Add the summer savory, pepper and salt.
3. In a separate medium pot, simmer the washed red lentils in 8 cups of water.
4. When the lentils are well cooked and lose their form, add them to the veggies and stir to combine.

Vegan Bolognese Sauce

Calactus

Preparation time: 40 minutes ~ Serves: 6 ~ Level of difficulty: 2.5 ~ S/F

Typical Bolognese sauce is a meaty pasta sauce that originated in Italy. This vegan version is hearty and easy to make. The dish reminds me of Mom's home cooking—satisfying and very similar to spaghetti sauce. The recipe calls for textured vegetable protein (TVP), a tasty and easy to find meat substitute that tastes so much like the real deal, if I hadn't told my guests they were eating vegan, they never would have known. I cook this with two packages of brown rice spaghetti noodles, which makes a healthy and simple meal for company.

Ingredients

1 large Spanish onion, diced
1 1/4 cups canola oil
1 1/4 tablespoons garlic, minced
1/2 of a medium green pepper, diced
1 pound mixed veggies, raw (diced zucchini, broccoli, carrots or veggies of choice)
2 cups water

1/2 tablespoon salt
1 teaspoon pepper
2 tablespoon oregano
3 cups of textured vegetable protein (TVP)
3 1/4 cups of organic tomato sauce
3 1/2 tablespoons of balsamic vinegar

Method

1. In a medium pot, sautée Spanish onion in canola oil until translucent and soft.
2. Add the garlic, green pepper and veggies, and sautée.
3. Add the water, salt, pepper and oregano.
4. Bring to a boil and remove from heat.
5. Add the TVP.
6. Stir, cover and let sit for 15 minutes.
7. Stir in organic tomato sauce and balsamic vinegar.

In my early 20s I decided I must discover the most exciting city on earth so I hopped on a bus going from Montreal to the great New York City. The bus flew through a long tunnel and busted out into the city.

That was the moment I fell in love with the city.

Incredible buildings competed around me, one seeming higher then the next and the energy was intensely exciting. I could wander the streets and continually be amused by the sights and people and excitement of fabulous New York City. As years went by I always came back to New York for several months at a time. I just could not entirely give up on living there... it was my first love.

I came home to New York for the second time when I was 22. This was just three weeks after I became vegan. How lucky was I discovering this diet in

New York, the most vegan friendly city in the world.

I planted myself in the hub of veganism, the East Village, where on every corner there's a bar and on the opposite corner a juice bar or vegetarian diner.

New York City is fast, hard, exciting and intoxicating.

My love for the city's vegan restaurants and yoga studios brought me the peace, caring and loving atmospheres that helped to balance the chaos of New York City life.

Hangawi

The Hangawi dining experience is an affair of all the senses.

Peaceful, traditional Korean atmosphere, meditative music, beautiful setting and perfect flavors. It's an escape from the chaos of New York City into delicious serenity and bliss.

honorable mentions

Recommended Restaurant
Michellin Guide 2013

Best Korean Restaurant from 1996 to 2012
Zagat New York City Restaurants

Awarded Certificate of Excellence for the year 2012
Trip Advisor

One of the 40 best restaurants in New York
Zagat New York City Restaurants

Best Korean restaurant in New York & Best Vegetarian
Zagat

Stuffed Mushrooms
Hangawi Restaurant

Cook time: 35 minutes ~ Serves: 4 ~ Level of difficulty: 3 ~ G/F

Hot fried mushrooms are one of my favorite things. These little wonders are fried golden brown on the outside, packed full of tasty stuffing and sitting in a delightful almond sauce. They're not overly complex to make and are a perfect appetizer at a dinner party as they are well-loved by all mushroom fans.

Ingredients

For the Shiitake Mushrooms and Stuffing:
8 medium sized Shiitake mushrooms
2 tablespoons carrot, minced
10 ounces medium firm tofu, minced
1/2 cup oyster mushrooms, minced
2 large tablespoons parsley, minced
3 tablespoons onion, minced
black pepper to taste
1 teaspoon sesame seeds
1 teaspoon mushroom powder (found in Asian markets or made by grinding mushrooms)
1/2 to 1/4 teaspoon salt2 tablespoons sesame oil
1 teaspoon ginger paste, or minced fresh ginger blended with a little water
1 teaspoon potato powder

For the Almond Sauce:
2 tablespoons almonds, chopped
2 tablespoons water
1 tablespoon mirin, or sweet rice wine
1/2 tablespoon agave syrup
1 tablespoon corn syrup
pinch of salt
oil for frying

Method

For the Stuffed Shiitake Mushrooms:
1. Mix the carrot, tofu, oyster mushrooms, parsley and onions in a large bowl.
2. Add black pepper, sesame seeds, mushroom powder, salt, sesame oil, ginger paste and potato powder and mix well.
3. Wash the shiitake mushrooms well and cut the stems away.
4. Make little patties with the ingredients in the bowl and stuff the patties in the shiitake mushrooms.
5. Heat a pan with the oil and pan fry the stuffed shitake mushrooms on both sides until golden brown.

For the Almond Sauce:
1. Blend the almonds with water, mirin or sweet rice wine, agave syrup, corn syrup and salt until the mixture becomes milky and consistent.
2. Drizzle the almond sauce onto a serving plate and arrange the Stuffed Shiitake Mushrooms on top.

Peacefood Cafe

Peacefood Cafe became part of New York City's smorgasbord of vegan restaurants in June, 2009. Quickly after opening, the restaurant became a bustling busy vegan hub. When I first heard of the place I had been in New York for a couple of years and could map out the trendiest and longest lasting vegan restaurants in the city. Over time, I was enticed by the restaurant's excellent reviews so I decided I must try it.

The orginal Peacefood Cafe is located in New York's Upper West Side, a calmer part of New York, offering a peaceful retreat from the hustle and bustle. It is a beautiful, bright, open space, warmly lit and complemented by a variety of artwork and live plants. The environment is casual and generally busy with patrons.

On my first review of the restaurant I arrived in the afternoon with a girlfriend who was a well-experienced vegan testee. We meet with Eric Yu, the owner. It quickly became clear why Peacefood has thrived in such a competitive city. Eric is a shining example of a foodie—a wonderful man who is enthusiastic about food and adores watching people enjoy their meals at his restaurant. I left Peacefood feeling incredibly full! I was impressed with the restaurant, the prices were reasonable and every dish tasted exceptional.

One of the items I tried was the famous Raw Key Lime Pie. It has a creamy, lime flavored filling and a sweet, dense perfect crust. Peacefood has included the recipe here, along with Quinoa Tabouli with French Horn Mushrooms and Roasted Garlic. This recipe contains light fluffy quinoa, peppery arugula and gorgeous fried mushroom and garlic flavors. If you are lucky enough to visit Peacefood Cafe, bring a big appetite, as there are many must-try items like Shanghai-style Dumplings, cooked to perfection and filled with chives, mushrooms and tofu and served with a delicious ginger balsamic dipping sauce. The award-winning Chick Pea Fries are exceptional, hot and crisp with a hint of Indian spice.

Peacefood's "Other Caeser" is my all-time favorite Caeser salad, served with crisp romaine, veggies, smoked tempeh and secret award winning dressing. I am also infatuated with the Roasted Potatoes Pizza, served with sautéed mushrooms, arugula, cured black olives and pesto.

Peacefood Cafe has become so popular, in March 2013 it opened a second location at 41 East 11th Street. The new Peacefood Cafe in the New York East Village will help to make the area a little tastier and the vegan foods lovers happier!

"Peace starts with the food that we eat, with what we put on our plate," said co-owner Eric Yu. *"If we go out and kill for our food, that disturbs nature, the law of the universe. That's not peaceful."*

Best Fries 2010 – Chick Pea Fries
Time Out magazine

Best Caesar Salad - Best Vegan Bites
The Vegan Guide to New York City

Best Veggie Burger – Eric's Jalapeño Daiya "Cheeseburger"
The Vegan Guide to New York City

Featured in TV segment WABC – **Neighborhood Eats: Raw Key Lime Pie**

Featured in TV segment WCBS Tony Tantillo's **Dining Deal**

Quinoa Tabouli

with French Horn Mushrooms and Roasted Garlic
Peacefood Cafe

In Advance: Pre-chill the tofu slices in the refrigerator for an hour, Cook broccoli and cauliflower and chill ~ Preparation time: 45 minutes ~ Serves: 6 ~ Level of difficulty: 3.5 ~ G/F

This is a delicious and light meal. The garlic is slowly cooked in the olive oil, which softens its flavor and flavors the oil. It blends well with the light fluffy quinoa, peppery arugula and gorgeous fried mushrooms. The dish is flavorful without being over powering and is healthy and satisfying.

Ingredients

2 cups of cooked quinoa

3/4 cup olive oil, divided

1 pound of French horn mushrooms, cut lengthwise into 1/4-inch thick slices

salt and pepper to taste

1 cup garlic cloves

1 block of extra firm tofu, cut into 1/4-inch thick slices and pre-chilled

3 tablespoons olive oil

1/2 cup red onion, diced

1 cup cooked or canned small white beans, drained and rinsed

2 cups broccoli and cauliflower florets, cooked and diced

sea salt flakes for tossing

10 cups baby arugula

Method

1. Pour 1/4 cup olive oil in skillet turn heat to medium. Add mushroom slices, season with salt and pepper to taste, and cook for about 20-25 until the mushrooms are crispy and brown. Stir often.
2. Transfer to a plate and cover.
3. Later, cut into 1/4 inch cubes if desired.
4. Pour 1/2 cup of olive oil in skillet on medium-low heat. Add garlic cloves and a pinch of salt. Cook the garlic about 15-20 minutes until it is soft and golden brown. Stir often. Set aside. Later drain and reserve oil, and cut garlic into small dices.
5. Drain water out of the tofu and pat dry with a towel.
6. Heat 3 tablespoons of olive oil in a pan over medium-high heat. Place tofu in a single layer, season with salt and pepper, and let stand for 4-5 minutes. Do not stir.
7. Turn the tofu over, and repeat the cooking process.
8. Transfer tofu to a plate and cover. Later cut them into 1/4 inch cubes.

Assembly

1. Mix all ingredients except the sea salt flakes in a large bowl. Add the sea salt flakes and some of the reserved oil from the garlic to taste. Squeeze fresh lemon over top if desired. Serve room temperature or cold.

Raw Key Lime Pie
Peacefood Cafe

In Advance: Soak cashews for 24 hours ~ Preparation time: 30 minutes ~ Freeze time: 2-3 hours ~ Serves: 12 ~ Level of difficulty: 3.5 ~ Equipment: Food processor ~ G/F & S/F

The first time I went to Peacefood I had a brief encounter with a customer by the juice bar. He promptly proclaimed his love for the Raw Key Lime Pie. Actually, he described it as the "famous" Key Lime Pie. He told me I must try it, and I replied with an instant pie order. I consumed mine in bliss via creamy lime filling and sweet, perfect pie crust. I was amazed once again by how delightful raw food could be. I was thrilled when Peacefood sent me the Raw Key Lime Pie recipe. It's rather pricey to make, especially if you are buying raw organic nuts, yet it is unique, healthy and so good! Use organic and raw nuts and unprocessed virgin oil to preserve its raw state. Enjoy!

Ingredients

For the Crust:
1 cup whole almonds
1 1/2 cup Brazil nuts
1/2 cup dates
pinch of salt
1/8 cup coconut oil, room temperature

For the Filling:
3/4 cup cashews, soaked
3/4 cup young coconut meat
3/4 cup agave
pinch of salt
3-6 limes, zested
3/4 cup fresh lime juice, reserved from zested limes
3 avocados
3/4 cup coconut oil
dried coconut and lime slices to garnish

Method

For the Crust:
1. Place the almonds, brazil nuts, dates and salt into the food processor. Process until the ingredients come together. Place in a small bowl.
2. Add the coconut oil and knead by hand until incorporated.
3. Form a thin crust in the glass pie dish. Set aside.

For the Filling:
1. Strain the water from the cashews and rinse.
2. Place the cashews, young coconut meat, agave and salt in the food processor and process until the mixture is very smooth. Add lime zest, lime juice and avocados.
3. Taste the mixture after you add half the lime zest, and adjust to taste.
4. Process until completely smooth, about 5-6 minutes.
5. Add coconut oil last and incorporate.

Assembly

1. Pour the filling into the crust and freeze for 2 to 3 hours. Pull from freezer and let the pie temper before serving.
2. Garnish with dried coconut and lime slices.

Quintessence

Quintessence is located in New York's East Village, a bohemian neighborhood with a great number of vegan and raw food restaurants.

I moved to the East Village in my early 20s when I was starting out on a plant-based diet. I had a fabulous life of dining during that time and experienced many incredible restaurants. Even with the fierce vegan competition in this borough, Quintessence comes out on top.

Quintessence is housed in a small, peaceful retreat in a city of intensity. The kind servers and friendly atmosphere often lead to interesting conversation and new friendships.

In 1999, Quintessence was one of North America's premier raw food restaurants. Dan Hoyt and co-founder Mun Chan used their creative talents and knowledge of health and wellness to open the restaurant. This was a time when raw culinary options were healthy but not particularly enticing. Dan used his culinary genius to create raw vegan food that tasted delicious and resembled familiar foods like pizza and burgers. This was a new concept that was very appealing to customers. Since then many raw food restaurants have copied this culinary style. Dan Hoyt would have people from across the country and around the world come to see what he was doing with raw food.

For most of its life Quintessence served only organic raw food; yet, in recent years has added a few cooked items. Quintessence has a globally inspired menu with many incredible dishes to choose from. Some of my favorite items include the Ravioli, which is made of paper-thin sliced turnips filled with sun-dried tomato basil and "cheese" served on yellow squash pasta with choice of rich tomato Napolitano or pesto sauce. With its full flavor and nice, creamy filling, each bite is incredible and leaves you feeling great. When in New York I am a regular lunchtime attendee, hooked on the lunch special, which includes a main, salad and tea or apple cider.

My current favorite is the Mock Tuna Sandwich, which uses the Mock Tuna Salad Recipe included in the book. The Mock Tuna Salad does a great job of resembling traditional tuna salad and is filling and energizing. I am also hooked on the Quintessence desserts and am thrilled to have the delicious Three Berry Pie. Quintessence calls the treats "guiltless desserts," a concept I fully endorse.

Quintessence was designed to be a gourmet dining retreat that satisfies the appetite and energizes, rejuvenates and refreshes from the inside out. It's a perfect oasis in an intoxicating city.

"Best Raw Food Restaurant"
Hippocrates

"Best Vegetarian Restaurant"
VegNews Magazine

"Love is a fruit in season at all times and within reach of every hand."

Mother Theresa

Raw Mock Tuna Salad
Quintessence

In Advance: Soak walnuts for six hours or overnight ~ Preparation time: 20 minutes ~ Serves: 2-4 ~ Level of difficulty: 2 ~ Equipment: Food processor with "S" blade ~ G/F & S/F

This recipe is a demonstration of Quintessence co-owner Chef Dan's culinary genius. The Mock Tuna Salad is so tasty and full of goodness—it's a must try. It does a good job of resembling tuna salad, yet is healthy and vitally good. If you want to keep this a raw dish, be sure to use raw walnuts and cold pressed extra virgin olive oil.

At Quintessence, this Mock Tuna Salad is a popular menu appetizer. They put it between two pieces of baby romaine leaves topped with chopped tomato, cucumber, avocado, raw mayo and mustard sauce.

Ingredients

2 cups walnuts, soaked and dried
1/4 cup dulse, chopped (dulse is a dark seaweed and
is available at health food stores)
1/4 cup parsley, chopped
1/2 bell pepper, chopped
1-2 cloves garlic, medium minced

2 tablespoons lemon juice
1/4 cup olive oil
1/2 teaspoon sea salt
1/4 cup celery, chopped
1/4 cup onion, chopped
1/4 cup dill, chopped

Method
1. Combine walnuts, dulse, parsley, bell pepper, garlic, lemon juice, olive oil and sea salt in the food processor using the "S" blade. Process until the mixture becomes creamy. Add water as needed, but keep it a thick paste.
2. Transfer the mixture to a mixing bowl and mix in celery, onion and dill with a fork. Serve at room temperature.

Raw Three Berry Pie

Quintessence

Preparation time: 40 minutes Level of difficulty: 3.5 ~ Serves: 8-10 ~ G/F & S/F

Sweet, fresh and delightful! This is one of the tastiest pies you can have and certainly one of the healthiest. Enjoy!

Ingredients

For the Crust:
1 cup almonds
1 cup sunflower seeds
8 dried apricots
1 teaspoon vanilla
1 teaspoon sea salt

For the Filling:
1 cup coconut flakes
1 cup pecans
4 medjool dates
2 teaspoons vanilla
2 teaspoons cinnamon
1 teaspoon nutmeg
1 teaspoon sea salt
raspberries, blueberries and chopped strawberries (as many as desired to fold into pie filling)

Method

For the Crust:
1. In a food processor, blend crust ingredients until sticky.
2. Press into a 9inch pie pan and set aside.

For the Filling:
1. Blend all ingredients except berries in a food processor.
2. Fold raspberries, blueberries and chopped strawberries in by hand.
3. Fill pie crust with the mixture (do not pack it in too tight) and refrigerate for 2 hours before serving.

Paris

Tommy's Restaurant

Tommy's has been one of the most popular establishments in the Coventry area, a bohemian neighborhood, since 1972. It is one of the few restaurants in Ohio that has been serving tofu since the 70s and with great success. Tommy's delicious vegan and vegetarian fare has been perfected in their decades of service. The perfection can be tasted in the bright, fresh flavors of the Pasta Salad and Tabouli recipes that Tommy has included in Best Vegan.

The tasty food is served in a family style restaurant as Tommy's children work there and his wife's beautiful touch can be seen through her art work displayed in the restaurant and on the adjacent page. If you have a chance to visit Tommy's you will find a bright, fun restaurant buzzing with popularity and filled with stories, memories and great flavors.

Tommy's Famous Guests

Adrian Grenier - Vince on HBO's Entourage   Alicia Keys – Singer   Alicia Silverstone – Actress   Anthony Bourdain - TV Chef   Anthony Geary & Genie Francis – 'Luke & Laura' - General Hospital   Anthrax – Musicians   – Actor Butch Patrick - 'Eddie Munster'   Calvin Hill - Football Player   Chyna Phillips – Actress   Billy Baldwin   Daniel Thompson - Poet   Dave Coulier - Comedian, Actor &   Danny DeVito   Voice Over Artist   Dave Patterson - News Anchor   David Moss - TV Personality Diane DiPrima – Author   Drew Carey – Actor Drew Lachey - Actor Sm Ketley - Cleveland Heights Mayor   Ellen Degeneris – Actress   Gay Marshall – Actress – Actress Jackson Browne - Musician Jayne Kennedy – Actress   Jim Fox - of the James Gang Jim Jarmusch - Movie Director JoAnne Woodward – Actress   Jonah Kosten – Singer Jonathan Richman & Tommy Larkins – Musicians Josh Cribbs - Football Player   LeBron James - Basketball Player   Lee Fisher – Politician   Les Levine - Sports Commentator Mekons – Musicians   Molly Shannon - of 'Saturday Night Live' Monica Potter - Actress   Mr. Stress (Bill Miller) - Musician   Ozzie Newsome - Football Player   Pardo Ponds - Musician Patty Smith – Singer   Heather Graham   Rachael Ray - TV Host   Regina Brett - Plain Dealer Columnist Sean Lennon – Musician   Sheryl Crow's band – Musicians   Sherrod Brown – Politician Sonic Youth - Musicians Stefani Schaefer - News Anchor   Steve Presser - of 'Big Fun' fame   Supertramp – Musicians   Susan Goldberg - Plain Dealer Editor   Taking Back Sunday – Musicians Ted Henry - News Anchor   Ted Neeley - Drummer, Singer, Actor & Composer

honorable mentions

The Silver Spoon Award
Cleveland Maganzine
Best Vegetarian Restaurant
Northern Ohio Live
Best Vegetarian Restaurant
Scene Magazine
Best Health Conscious Menu
Northern Ohio Live

Pasta Salad
with Creamy Vinegar Plum Dressing
Tommy's Restaurant

Preparation time: 25 minutes ~ Serves: 2 ~ Level of difficulty: 2 ~ Equipment: Blender

This pasta salad puts classic, non-vegan pasta salad to shame. It's healthier, more interesting and tastier. I made this recipe when I received it and can't stop making it because I keep getting requests for it. It boasts a mixture of bright vegetable and olive flavors along with a delicious Creamy Vinegar Plum Dressing. It's a hit! Classic pasta salad is served cold so you may want to cool the noodles prior to serving. I use brown rice rotini shaped pasta noodles, which are healthy and taste great.

Ingredients

For the Pasta Salad:
2 cups cooked pasta
1/2 cup carrot sticks
1/2 cup broccoli florets, steamed
1/4 cup celery, green peppers and seedless cucumbers, diced
1/4 cup red onions, finely chopped
1/4 cup olives, sliced

For the Dressing:
1 clove garlic, minced
1/2 cup olive oil
1/4 cup brown rice vinegar
1 tablespoon fresh lemon juice
1 tablespoon umebosi plum paste, found in Japanese markets

Method

For the Dressing:
1. Put all ingredients in a blender and pulse until smooth.

For the Pasta Salad:
1. Combine pasta salad ingredients in a large bowl.
2. Add desired amount of dressing and mix thoroughly.

Tabouli

Tommy's Restaurant

Preparation time: 35 minutes, 15-35 minutes to soak bulgur wheat ~ Serves: 4 ~ Level of difficulty: 2 ~ S/F

This is a vibrant and flavourful Middle Eastern dish. It includes bulgur wheat, which is a healthy cereal grain that is high in fibre and essential to traditional tabouli recipes. Sometimes I switch the bulgur wheat for quinoa, which makes it a high protein meal.

Ingredients

For the Salad:
2 cups parsley, finely chopped
2 cups green onions, finely chopped
1/4 cup fresh mint, finely chopped
1 cup ripe tomatoes, fine-medium chopped
1/2 cup cracked dry bulgar wheat
wheat pita and romaine lettuce as a side

For the Dressing:
1/2 cup olive oil
1/2 cup lemon
1/4 teaspoon salt

Method

1.Soak the bulgur wheat in 1 cup of boiled water, covered, for 15-35 minutes. Drain the excess water from the bulgur when it seems to have expanded and then fluff with a fork
2. In a large bowl, combine the prepared bulgar with the rest of the salad ingredients.
3. Wisk together the dressing ingredients and pour over the prepared Tabouli.
4. Serve cold on a bed of romaine leaves with a side of toasted wheat pita.

Toronto, Ontario

Live Organic Food Bar

Live Organic Food Bar will feed you an incredible meal and leave you with more energy and a better day than you arrived with. The restaurants are friendly places that serve a mostly raw menu with ingenious recipes. Internationally known Chef Jennifer Italiano takes her deep love of food and health and creates exceptional vegan dishes.

The menu flaunts an array of salads, wraps, burgers, bowls, appetizers, treats and mains that are internationally inspired. Jennifer's creativity and talents can be tasted through the Kelp Noodle Salad recipe included in Best Vegan. With its creamy Thai flavors, it is fresh and energizing. The Raw Sushi recipe is incredible. The slightly sweet base is complemented by the salty, crunchy raw "tempura," which is left with the cilantro, lemon and garlic flavors. These recipes show off the restaurant's beautiful taste and healthful dishes.

Live Organic Food Bar describes its culinary practice: "We believe that the only way food should be processed is by the human body. Our cuisine is influenced by the flavors we remember from our mother's kitchen. Many different cultural ingredients are combined in our hand-made, organic, vegan dishes where quality and flavor come first."

With love, caring and talent Live Organic Food Bar feeds our minds, bodies and souls.

Best of Canada Organic/Healthy Restaurant
People's Choice 2012~ NaturalHealthCare.ca

Jennifer Italiano - Best of Toronto - Insider Insights
NOW- Toronto

9 of Dine Chefs of Distinction Awards
Gourmet Food/Wine Expo

"A hero is someone who has given his or her life to something bigger than oneself."

Joseph Campbell

Raw Kelp Noodle Salad

Live Organic Food Bar

Preparation time: 30 minutes ~ Serves: 2-4 ~ Level of difficulty: 3 ~ Equipment: Blender~S/F ~ G/F

A note from Live Organic Food Bar:

This Thai-inspired, beautiful noodle salad is bursting with flavor and nutrition. The sauce is creamy, a little limey, and a little spicy. The recipe contains kelp noodles, which are readily available at health food stores and Asian markets. High in minerals and vitamins, kelp balances the body's Ph levels, while providing other benefits. Super food maca, also found at health food stores, will give you fuel for the day. This sauce can be used on pasta or rice. Enjoy!

Ingredients

For the Sauce:
1 cup of almond butter
2 tablespoons ginger, chopped
5 cloves of garlic
1/2 red onion
1 1/2 red peppers
2 small carrots
1 1/2 Thai chillies or jalapenos
1/4 cup of rice vinegar
1/2 cup lime juice
2 tablespoons agave nectar
1 tablespoons of maca, optional
Celtic sea salt to taste

For the Salad:
1 bag of kelp noodles
1/2 package of enoki mushrooms, ends cut off and separated
1 bunch of dandelion greens (chiffonade)
1 red pepper, julienned
1 red onion, julienned
1 bunch of cilantro, lightly chopped
sunflower sprouts or almonds for garnish

Method

1. Blend all Sauce ingredients together until smooth.
2. Place all of the mixed vegetables in a large bowl and add the kelp noodles.
3. Add the sauce and toss to combine.
3. Garnish with sunflower sprouts or almonds and serve.

Tip: This recipe will make extra sauce. Consider saving some to use over rice or pasta or as a dip.

Raw Pecan Sushi with Tempura

& Miso Glaze
Live Organic Food Bar

In Advance: Dehydrate the tempura for 8 hours, soak pecans and sunflower seeds for a minimum of 4 hours

Preparation time: 40 minutes ~ Serves: 2-4 ~ Level of difficulty: 3 ~ Equipment: Dehydrator, Food processor, Blender ~ G/F & S/F

I made this sushi. My boyfriend took a few bites. He then spoke, "I am going to ask for this one again!" My friend had a few pieces and said it was the best sushi he ever had. Conclusion? It's exceptional!

The tempura is crispy and a little salty, and the pate is the perfect complement with a slightly sweet flavor highlighted with hints of cilantro, lemon and garlic. Wrap it all together with the sweetened miso glaze for little morsels of raw, vegan heaven.

Ingredients

For the Tempura:
1 sweet potato, peeled and shredded
2 tablespoons olive oil
Celtic sea salt and pepper to taste

For the Pecan Pate:
1 clove of garlic
1/4 cup dates, pitted
1 cup pecans, soaked
1/2 cup sunflower seeds, soaked
2 tablespoons lemon juice
2 tablespoons olive oil
Celtic sea salt to taste
pinch of cayenne
1/4 bunch of cilantro

For the Miso Glaze:
1/4 cup brown rice miso
1/2 teaspoon sesame oil
1/8 cup maple syrup
1 teaspoon rice vinegar
1 teaspoon tamari
water to blend

For the Sushi:
1 package of Nori seaweed sheets, used to wrap sushi
vegetables of your choice, cut into thin strips
pickled ginger for garnish

Method

For the Tempura:
1. Toss the sweet potato in olive oil and season with Celtic sea salt and pepper.
2. Place in dehydrator at 115 degrees F for 8 hours until crispy.

For the Pecan Pate:
1. Blend the garlic and dates in the food processor with a bit of water until they form a paste.
2. Add the remaining ingredients, except the cilantro, and mix until creamy.
3. Add the cilantro and pulse until blended in but not over-processed.

For the Miso Glaze:
1. Place all ingredients into blender and mix well. Set aside.

Assembly

1. Place 1/2 cup Pecan Pate on one sheet of nori. Top with dehydrated sweet potato and veggies of your choice.
2. Roll tightly and moisten the ends to seal the wrap.
3. Cut into sushi pieces using a sharp knife.
4. Drizzle miso glaze on a serving plate and place the sushi. Serve with pickled ginger.

Grasslands

Grasslands is located on QueenStreet West in Toronto, the city's trendiest block. The street is the location of the city's top boutiques, hip bars and clubs and the studio for the popular TV show, *MuchMusic*. The location is well suited to Grasslands, a stunning upscale restaurant. Patrons are greeted with a 30 foot bar constructed from live edge Ontario maple. Diners are seated in chocolate faux leather puckered booths and live edge tables. Local and craft brews are on tap and gluten-free beers are available by the bottle. Tear drop wooden pendants hang from the antique copper ceiling.

The vision for Grasslands, Toronto's first high-end vegan restaurant, came from Chef Gardner, who is a well known culinary genius. He has put his special touch into each of his vegan restaurants, three Urban Herbivore locations and Grasslands. Chef Gardner has won numerous awards for Best Cookies and Sandwiches, Best Veg Restaurants and for serving the city's Best Brunch. Grasslands gives him the opportunity to take his culinary skill to the next level with high-end innovative affair.

The menu offers tasty vegan dishes, many of which are inspired by northern Mediterranean cuisine. It flaunts a large variety of fresh salads, faux meat dishes and excellent pasta dishes. The bar pours from a great wine list and mixes classic cocktails like the Old Fashioned and French Martini. Grasslands is a place to indulge in incredible flavors, a beautiful setting and innovative excellence.

"The way is not in the sky. The way is in the heart."

Buddha

Chocolate Ganache

Grasslands

Preparation time: 15 minutes ~ Cooling time: 30 minutes ~ Yields: 15 chocolates ~ Level of difficulty: 2

Equipment: Food processor, Double boiler or pot and metal bowl, Plastic chocolate mould or flexible ice cube tray~ G/F

These lovely chocolates are rich and creamy with a hint of liqueur. They can only be described as perfect, darling little devils. They are easy to make, delivering gourmet chocolate flavor. Perfectly petite so you do not have to over-indulge. That is, if you can possibly eat just one!

Ingredients

1 ripe avocado
3 tablespoons of Jack Daniels sour mash whiskey
14 ounces (400 grams) dark chocolate
fruit and powdered sugar to garnish

Method

1. Puree avocado in food processor with the whiskey. Set aside in food processor.
2. Melt the chocolate in the double boiler or bring a small pot of water to a boil and place the chocolate in a medium sized metal bowl over the boiling water. Stir the chocolate constantly as it melts.
3. Pour the melted chocolate into the food processor with the pureed avocado and blend.
4. Pour the chocolate mixture into the plastic chocolate mould or flexible ice-cube trays.
5. Chill in the fridge for 1/2 an hour.
Serve with fruit and garnish with powdered sugar.

Celery Root Crème Sauce

Grasslands

In Advance: Prepare Roasted Garlic (recipe on page 136) ~ Preparation time: 25 minutes ~ Cook time: 20 minutes ~ Serves: 2 ~ Level of difficulty: 2 ~ Equipment: Blender ~ G/F & S/F

This creamy white wine pasta sauce is a little gift from recipe heaven. Its flavor is superb, healthy and delicious, and fairly easy to make. What a treat! Mix it with some brown rice noodles to create a nutritious, delightful pasta dish.

Tip: Celery root, also known as celeriac, is not found at every grocery store. Call ahead to a market with a diverse selection of food to check if they carry it. Celery root looks like a roundish white and brown root about the size of a softball, with some green stems growing from it.

Ingredients

3 cups of water
1 celery root, cut into 1-inch cubes
1/2 cup leeks, chopped
1/8 cup Roasted Garlic (recipe on page 136)

1/4 cup olive oil
1/2 cup white cooking wine
fresh basil, julienned and thyme leaves to garnish
salt and pepper to taste

Method

1. Bring the water to a boil in a small saucepan.
2. Add the celery root and leek and simmer for 14 minutes until tender.
3. Remove from the heat and drain the water.
4. Transfer to a blender. Add the garlic, oil and white cooking wine. Blend until smooth.
5. Season with salt and pepper to taste. Add the herbs just before serving.

The Green Door Restaurant

L-O-V-E (local, organic, vegetarian, eco-conscious) are the edible ideals that fuel the The Green Door Restaurant.

Those ideals, turned into tasty healthy meals, have been a hit since The Green Door Restaurant opened in 1988. It is the oldest and most popular vegetarian restaurant in Ottawa.

The restaurant is 1,800 square feet of space that seats 100 people and is regularly packed. The atmosphere is casual with a self-serve buffet, ever-changing local artwork and large tables that often lead to table sharing and interesting conversations with fellow customers.

After choosing what you like at the buffet you pay by weight. Many items change seasonally, yet you can always find some of the restaurant's tastiest specialties. The Green Door serves some of the best thick and juicy lasagna around, and there are always healthy varieties of fresh baked breads like spelt or rye, and a massive salad selection to mix and match.

The food is wholesome. The restaurant does not batter, over sweeten or fry away the fresh flavors of veggies and healthy products. The exceptional tastes of The Green Door are flaunted in Marinated Baked Tofu Salad, which is delicious and contains healthy, simple ingredients. The veggies are drizzled in flavorful sesame oil, lemon and tamari and the baked tofu is marinated to delight. The Fiddle Head Curry recipe makes an attractive dish, flavored with Indian spices.

Simple, local, healthy and, best of all, delicious has packed The Green Door Restaurant full of patrons for decades.

Bon Appetit!

Fiddlehead and Potato Curry
The Green Door Restaurant

Preparation time: 40 minutes ~ Serves: 6 ~ Level of difficulty: 3 ~ S/F & G/F

Fiddlehead and Potato Curry is a great meal that contains the spices of India, flavors of fried onion and hints of garlic, tasty potatoes and pretty fiddleheads, which have a flavor similar to asparagus. Fiddleheads harvest in mid to late spring and can be found at some grocers or farmers' markets. Loaded with healthful properties such as iron and potassium, the fiddleheads make this curry a satisfying, healthy meal.

Ingredients

3 tablespoons olive oil
pinch of asafetida
1/2 teaspoon ground cumin
1 teaspoon ground coriander
1 teaspoon garam masala
a pinch of ground cardamom
1 teaspoon ground turmeric
2 cloves garlic, crushed
2 cups onions, diced
1/4 teaspoon salt

1 heaping tablespoon fresh jalapeño, finely chopped, chili pepper, or cayenne to taste, starting with 1/4 teaspoon
1 medium sized tomato, diced
1 cup water
4 cups potatoes, diced into small chunks
4 cups fiddleheads, blanched (to blanche put in boiling water for 1 min. then put in cold water for 1 minute)
fresh cilantro and diced tomato for garnish

Method

1. Heat the olive oil in a large pot on low heat. Add the asafetida, cumin, coriander, garam masala, cardamom and turmeric and cook, stirring, for about 5 minutes.
2. Add garlic, onions and salt and cook until the onions are wilted.
3. Add the chili pepper, water, tomato and potatoes. Cook until the potatoes are done, about 20 to 25 minutes.
4. Add the fiddleheads.
5. Taste and adjust the salt if necessary.
6. Garnish with fresh cilantro and diced tomato.

Marinated Baked Tofu Salad

The Green Door Restaurant

In Advance: Marinate tofu for 6 hours or overnight ~ Preparation time: 45 minutes ~ Serves: 2 ~ Level of difficulty: 2.5 ~ G/F

Marinating and baking the tofu gives it a wonderful flavor. The dressing is a perfect blend of flavorful sesame oil, citrus lemon and salty tamari. This recipe is easy to make and light.

Ingredients

For the Tofu:
1 17 ounce (500 gram) block firm tofu, sliced width-wise into 8 slabs

For the Marinade:
1 1/4 cups water
2 large cloves garlic, crushed
1/4 cup tamari

For the Salad:
1/2 cup carrot, sliced in thin diagonals
1/2 cup celery, sliced in thin diagonals
1/4 cup whole green onions, sliced in thin diagonals
1 cup parsley, fine diced
1/4 cup arame seaweed, soaked for 5 minutes in warm water, drained

For the Dressing:
2 tablespoons dark sesame oil
2 tablespoons tamari
2 tablespoons freshly squeezed lemon juice
1 teaspoon brown rice vinegar
1 teaspoon ginger root, grated
1/2 teaspoon mirin or sweet rice wine
1 clove garlic, crushed

Method

For the Marinated Tofu:
1. Mix all marinade ingredients together in a bowl.
2. Place tofu slabs in the bowl, ensuring each slab is completely covered in marinade.
3. Cover the bowl and leave in the fridge for at least 6 hours or overnight.

For the Baked Tofu and Salad:
1. Pre-heat oven to 375 degrees F.
2. Drain the tofu from the marinade. Lay the tofu slices, not overlapped, on the prepared baking sheet.
3. Bake for 20 minutes, or until they are lightly browned.
4. Flip over and bake for another 15-20 minutes. The tofu slices will be light brown in color and slightly puffed.
5. Let the tofu cool and cut it into 1/2 inch strips.
6. Whisk together the Dressing ingredients
7. Place the tofu and vegetables in a large bowl. Pour the dressing over them, toss to combine and serve.

Portland

Portland is a pretty, friendly, laid-back city. It is also a little odd and funky, which people love. The popular saying, "Keep Portland weird," is a commitment to the city. Here, they cover locals in tattoos and piercings, and fill the bars with punk rock and the restaurants with amazing veggie food. It's a wonderful city with a wild spirit and a sweet, caring soul.

Oregon

egon produces heaps of fresh hazelnuts, potatoes, cherries and pears. *The countryside is full of beautiful tulip* farms, wine vineyards and coastal beaches making the state a spectacular site!

Blossoming Lotus

Walking into Blossoming Lotus I find warm, calm energy in this bright environment which buzzes with popularity. The restaurant's design is very simple, yet chic and comfortable. There are booths along the walls, plants in the front, which bask in sunlight through the large front windows.

The Blossoming Lotus serves all vegan food with a great selection of live food, gluten-free and seasonal items. They are well known for a fantastic brunch and on my first trip to the restaurant I tried the brunch special, the Crème Tofu Scramble. Bite by bite I was in heaven.

The Scramble was creamy with a cheesy flavor and filled with the flavors of fennel leak and fresh herbs. They included the recipe in Best Vegan, along with the Pumpkin Spice French Toast recipe—the best I have tried.

Made with fresh honey oat bread and cooked until golden brown, it has the perfect amount of sweetness with hints of coconut and cinnamon.

Each dish presented at Blossoming Lotus offers perfection, which has led to its great fame and reputation in the city. It's a local's treasure and a gift to travelers!

"delicious, creative, beautiful food"

Positively Vegan (blog)

Cheap Eats 2012 Award

Willamette Week

Best Casual Restaurant

VegNews Veggie Awards 2012

Wild Mushroom Tofu Scramble

with Leeks and Fennel in a Fresh Herb Cashew Crème
Blossoming Lotus

In advance: Soak cashews 6 hours or overnight ~ Preparation time: 30 minutes ~ Level of difficulty: 3 ~ Serves: 4 ~ Equipment: Blender ~ G/F

This is a lovely experience. It looks similar to a scramble egg breakfast and has a creamy, cheesy element. This creaminess is complemented by the perfect amount of flavorful veggies creating an impressive and cravable breakfast. Regardless of all its other tempting qualities, who would ever want to resist something that involves cashew crème sauce?

Ingredients

1 cup raw cashews, soaked
filtered water
2 tablespoons sunflower or other light cooking oil
salt
1 large leek, white part only, cleaned and chopped
1 bulb fennel, fronds and core removed, cleaned and julienned

1 block firm or extra firm tofu, water pressed out
4-5 ounces wild mushroom mix, cleaned and sliced
5 sprigs parsley, chopped + leaves for garnish
5 sprigs oregano, chopped
3 sprigs sage, chopped
sea salt and black pepper to taste
filtered water
1/4 cup nutritional yeast

Method

For the Cashew Crème:
1. Place soaked, drained, and rinsed cashews in a blender with enough filtered water to just cover them. Blend until completely smooth.

For the Tofu Scramble:
1. Heat a large skillet on medium heat. Add the oil and just a little salt.
2. Once oil is hot, add the mushrooms, leeks and fennel. Stir to completely coat the vegetables in oil. Cook until the mushrooms are slightly under-cooked, stirring frequently.
3. Crumble the tofu into the pan using your hands; the chunks should be no more than 1 inch.
4. Stir to fully incorporate the mushroom mixture and tofu. Continue to cook on medium heat, stirring frequently, until the tofu achieves a golden brown color.
5. Add the nutritional yeast and mix completely. At this point, the tofu should resemble scrambled eggs.

Pumpkin Spice French Toast
Blossoming Lotus

Preparation time: 20 minutes ~ Serves: 4 ~ Level of difficulty: 2

"Every morning when I get up, the first thing I decide is: What do I want? Misery? Blissfulness? What am I going to choose today? And it happens that I always choose blissfulness. It is my choice, it is my life." ~ Abdullah

For a bite of blissfulness, I recommend this Pumpkin Spice French Toast. It is golden brown, slightly sweet, and completely delicious. I made this for my boyfriend for breakfast and later that day he asked for it for dinner. It's a hit! It is also an inexpensive, impressive breakfast that's easy to put together for a group. Make it with fresh, baked, wholesome bread for an extra bite of health and happiness.

Ingredients

2 cups coconut milk
1/3 cup pumpkin puree (canned is acceptable, frozen is better, fresh is best)
1 scant teaspoon cinnamon, freshly grated
1/4 teaspoon nutmeg, freshly grated
1 teaspoon cornstarch
2 tablespoons agave syrup or equivalent
1 scant teaspoon liquid lecithin (available in most health food stores)

neutral cooking oil or margarine
8 slices any fresh or day old bread. Blossoming Lotus uses golden honey wheat and oat bread from a local baker.

Serve With:
Seasonal fruits
Your choice of quality syrup

Method

1. Place all batter ingredients in a blender, and blend until smooth.
2. Cut the bread into 1 inch thick slices.
3. Dip each slice of bread into the batter and allow to them to soak for 20 to 30 seconds.
4. Fry the prepared bread over medium heat in a thick bottomed sauté pan or cast iron skillet until golden brown. This should take about 3 to 4 minutes on each side.
5. Serve warm with seasonal fruit and your choice of quality syrup.

Nutrional Tip: Real maple syrup is made from the sap of the sugar maple tree, Acer saccharum. *Imitation syrup is typically made from a high fructose corn syrup base with food coloring and artificial flavors added.*

Real maple syrup contains compounds called phenolics, which may have a protective effect against cancer. Other phytochemicals in maple syrup include the antioxidants coumarin, vanillin, syringaldehyde and gallic acid, which neutralize free radicals that could harm cells.

Vita Café

Vita Café is a trendy place to hit up in the ultimate trendsetter city. The restaurant was born in 1999 and has developed into a delicious hit.

Vita Cafe has a large menu with American, Mexican, Asian and Middle Eastern-inspired entrées; both herbivores and carnivores can find something they will enjoy. The restaurant serves mainly vegan food and two of my all time favorite meals come from Vita Café. My choice breakfast is the Thai Corncakes. These are gluten-free cakes bursting with flavors of cilantro, ginger and banana and are smothered with lovely coconut syrup. These are an amazing way to start your day! Fortunately we can all do that as Vita Café included the recipe in Best Vegan.

The restaurant also included the Super Grain Salad with Fakin' Bacon and Lemon Tahini Dressing recipe, which is another main stay recipe on the menu. It's a filling salad with a quinoa and lettuce base and is filled with veggies, toasted pumpkins seeds, currants, avocado and a very nice Lemon Tahini Dressing. Best of all it includes the tastiest Fakin' Bacon I have discovered. The restaurant also serves a large variety of organic and non-organic vegan wines, beers and cocktails.

Vita Café has not forgotten to make an impact on the environment. The establishment's philosophy is to protect our world and the Portlanders by using as much local and organic produce as possible. Vita Café focuses on sustainable business practices. The restaurant is committed to purchasing 100% of its power from renewable energy sources such as wind, solar and biomass.

The restaurant has an honorable mandate and an extremely tempting aspect... incredible food. Vita Café is divine, creative, tasty and a vegan haven.

Japanese Gardens Portland, Oregon

Super Grain Salad

with Fakin' Bacon and Lemon Tahini Dressing
Vita Café

In Advance: Marinate Fakin' Bacon for several hours or overnight ~ Preparation time: 35 minutes ~ Serves: 4 ~ Level of difficulty: 3 ~ Equipment: Food processor (optional)

Fabulous, delicious, divine, healthy and amazing—this is another must make. It's a superb salad. Everything comes together so well—the quinoa adds a light flavor and is full of protein; the lettuce is crisp; the pumpkin seeds add saltiness and the Fakin' Bacon brings a smokiness complemented by the creamy avocado and Lemon Tahini Dressing. Perfection!

Ingredients

For the Fakin' Bacon:
1 pound tempeh
1 cup maple syrup
2 cups soy sauce
1/4 cup liquid smoke
1 tablespoon black pepper
1/2 cup water

For the Lemon Tahini Dressing:
1/2 cup lemon juice
1/4 cup tahini paste
2 tablespoons vegan sugar
1 teaspoon coarse black pepper
1 teaspoon sea salt
zest of 1 small lemon
3/4 cup olive oil

For the Super Grain Salad:
1 head green leaf lettuce, washed, dried and chopped
1 romaine heart, washed, dried and chopped
1 pound toasted, salted pepitas (pumpkin seeds)
2 cups quinoa, cooked and cooled
1 pound dried currants (or raisins)
1 red bell pepper, julienned
1 avocado, quartered and sliced

Method

For the Fakin' Bacon Crumbles:
1. Dice the tempeh into 1/2 inch cubes.
2. Mix all ingredients together in a large bowl, making sure the tempeh is completely submerged in the marinade.
3. Cover and store in refrigerator for several hours (ideally overnight).
4. Remove tempeh from the marinade and bake at 350 degrees F for 10 minutes or until crispy.

For the Lemon Tahini Dressing:
1. Put all ingredients except the olive oil into a mixing bowl.
2. Whisk well, then slowly drizzle in the olive oil to emulsify.
3. Store covered in the refrigerator for up to seven days.

Helpful Tip: This dressing can be made in a blender or food processor for a thicker, creamier consistency.

For the Super Grain Salad:
1. Combine all ingredients in a large bowl. Add the the Fakin' Bacon snd Lemon Tahini Dressing and serve.

Thai Corn Cakes

Vita Café

Preparation time: 35 minutes ~ Yields: 8 cakes ~ Level of difficulty: 3 ~ G/F

Do yourself a favor and wake up to these exotic, fantastic, better than pancake wonders. The recipe calls for masa harina, a flour used in Mexican cooking that can be found at a Mexican grocer or in the baking aisle of some supermarkets. The creamy coconut syrup is poured over the corn cakes, complementing the cilantro, ginger and sweet banana flavors.

Ingredients

For the Thai Corn Cakes:
8 tablespoons Earth Balance, or other vegan butter substitute
2 cups fine grind corn meal
1 1/4 cups rice flour or other gluten-free flour
3/4 cup masa harina
1/2 tablespoon baking powder
2 teaspoons sea salt
2 teaspoons vegan sugar
1/4 cup maple syrup

1/4 cup applesauce
3 cups water
2 bananas, sliced
1/4 cup ginger, ground or grated
1/2 bunch cilantro, washed and chopped

For the Coconut Syrup:
13.5 ounce can coconut milk
1/4 cup brown sugar
2 tablespoons cornstarch

Method

For the Thai Corn Cakes:
1. In a small saucepan, melt the Earth Balance on medium heat. Set aside to cool.
2. Mix all dry ingredients, the next 6, in a mixing bowl.
3. Mix the cooled Earth Balance and all wet ingredients, the next 3, in a separate large mixing bowl.
4. Thoroughly whisk dry ingredients into wet ingredients, making sure to scrape any settled dry mix from the bottom.
5. Heat a lightly greased skillet or flat bottomed pan over medium heat.
6. Ladle out corn cake batter onto skillet into cakes about 5 inches in diameter.
7. Place banana slices, ginger and cilantro into the cakes.
8. Cook for about 5 minutes, or until the top edges begin to solidify.
9. Flip and cook for an additional 5 minutes.
10. Give them a poke to make sure they are cooked through. Remove from skillet and serve with warm Coconut Syrup.

For the Coconut Syrup:
1. Whisk all ingredients together in a medium bowl.
2. Pour into a sauté pan and cook over medium heat until the syrup begins to simmer and slightly thicken.
3. Reduce the heat and simmer for an additional 5 minutes, whisking continuously.
4. Drizzle over Thai Corn Cakes.

Elfreth's Alley Philadelphia

Snowy cold winters, blossoming springs, hot humid
summers and golden leaf falls
Pennsylvania offers diversity in seasons, cultures and landscapes.

A energizing, sharp East Coast vibe hits the cities of Philadelphia and Pittsburgh

filling them with the arts, sports, fabulous restaurants, fun people and fastpaced lives.

Pennsylvania farmers produce more mushrooms than any other state with annual production of 443 million pounds. Winter wheat and buckwheat are important crops in the state as well. Pennsylvania also grows apples, cherries, peaches and grapes.

Vedge Restaurant

Vedge Restaurant is housed in the historic Tiger Building on trendy Locust Street in Philadelphia. The restaurant is known as one of top high-end vegan restaurants in the world and one of the best restaurants in Philadelphia. Vedge offers elegant dining with bold flavors and a progressive, seasonal menu.

Creative vegan delicacies splash Vedge's menu like the Spicy Grilled Tofu, Wood Roasted Turnips, Chocolate Uber Chunk Dessert and Sweet Pomegranate Sangria. The beautiful flavors of a Vedge meal can be tasted in the Pastrami Spiced Young Carrots recipe, which flaunts spicy sweet carrots and a bold Chickpea Sauerkraut Puree. Chef and owner Richard Landau displays genius through the Mushroom Pho Soup, which is lightly spiced and packed with delicious mushrooms. Richards's wife Kate is responsible for the innovative dessert menu. Here one finds classics like the Sticky Tofu Pudding, which is made special with its sweet brown sugar-date cake, and creamy cold Smoked Pecan Ice Cream.

Vedge restaurant inspires creativity, delivers great taste and offers an elegant experience.

honorable mentions

Chef Rich Landau wins Chopped
Food Network

Outstanding Restaurants of 2013 Vegan Restaurants in America
Shape Magazine

Best Chef
Philadelphia Magazine

12 Most Outstanding Restaurants of 2013
GQ Magazine

50 Best Restaurants
Philadelphia Magazine

Vedge Wins Produce Innovation Award
Cooking Light Magazine

Vedge awarded one of the top 10 upscale vegan restaurants in America
Shape Magazine

Pastrami Spiced Young Carrots

with Chick Pea Sauerkraut Puree
Vedge

Preparation time: 35 minutes ~ Serves: 4-6 ~ Level of difficulty: 3 ~ Equipment: Food processor ~ S/F & G/F

Vedge's Chef Jeffery Lapadula calls this recipe a fun, vegetable-only take on sausage & sauerkraut with Eastern European flavors. The spices play against the carrots' sweetness beautifully, and when enjoyed with the Chick Pea Sauerkraut Puree it recalls a Reuben. The recipe can be served hot or cold.

Ingredients

2 pounds of young or baby bunch carrots (or baby peeled carrots)
4 tablespoons olive oil
2 teaspoons sherry vinegar
2 tablespoons Montreal steak seasoning
1/2 teaspoon clove, ground
1 to 2 teaspoons salt
1 to 2 teaspoons black pepper

2 teaspoons fresh garlic, crushed
2 tablespoons Dijon mustard
1 12 ounce can of garbanzo beans (chick peas), drained
3/4 cup canned or jarred sauerkraut with some of its juice
2 tablespoons fresh dill

Tip: Reduce the salt to 1 teaspoon if the chickpeas are salted.

Method

1. Pre-heat oven to 350 degrees F.
2. Peel the carrots if necessary and trim the tops if they are attached. If you like, leave on about an inch of stem for a nice visual effect. Toss in 2 tablespoons of the olive oil, sherry vinegar, Montreal steak spice, clove, 1/2 to 1 teaspoon each of the salt and pepper, and 1 teaspoon of the garlic.
3. Spread the prepared carrots on a sheet pan, cover with foil and roast for 10-15 minutes or until they are just about tender. Remove the foil and roast uncovered for 3-5 minutes or until the carrots are almost soft. Remove from the oven and allow to cool.
4. Meanwhile, combine the remaining ingredients in a food processor and puree to a smooth, hummus-like puree. Add water to thin the mixture if necessary.
5. Place carrots on serving plates, top with Chick Pea Sauerkraut Puree and serve.

Mushroom Pho

Vedge

Preparation time: 40 minutes ~ Serves: 6 ~ Level of difficulty: 3 ~ S/F & G/F

This is absolutely delicious Pho soup. It has an incredible broth, which is a little spicy with delicious mushroom flavours. The soup is Vedge's vegetarian take on the classic Vietnamese beef soup. It's bursting with mushrooms, fresh veggies and rice noodles, all of which make it a light, healthy and satisfying Pho meal. It takes lots of mushrooms and a bit of time, but is well worth the benefits.

Ingredients

For the Broth:
3 tablespoons sesame oil
1/2 cup onion, roughly chopped
2 tablespoons garlic, roughly chopped
2 pounds mushroom trimmings, portabella and shiitake stems, maitake bases
8 ounces dried shiitakes (optional for extra depth)
2 teaspoons rice wine vinegar
12 cups water
2 tablespoons fresh ginger, chopped, peel on
4 whole star anise
2 whole cinnamon sticks
1 tablespoons 5 spice powder, preferably Vietnamese style
1/2 cup tamari

To Finish the Pho:
3 8 ounce packages of medium wide rice noodles
1 pound maitake or shiitake mushrooms
1 tablespoon toasted sesame oil
1 teaspoon each salt and pepper
1 pound fresh baby bok choy, Chinese broccoli or spinach, chopped
1 bunch of cilantro, chopped
1/2 bunch of scallion, green part only, sliced thinly on a diagonal
1/2 pound bean sprouts
Sriracha to taste, approximately 1 teaspoon per serving (commonly found in Asian aisle of the grocery store)

Method

For the Broth:
1. In a large stockpot on high heat, bring the sesame oil up to almost smoking.
2. Add the onion, ginger and mushroom trimmings.
3. Brown for 3-5 minutes, then add the rice wine vinegar.
4. When the rice wine evaporates, add the water and the remaining ingredients. Simmer on medium low for approximately 45 minutes or until the liquid has reduced by half.
5. Strain the broth into a plastic bucket or bowl.

For the Finish:
1. Pre-blanch the noodles by dipping them in boiling water for 5-45 seconds until they soften, then drain and rinse under cold water. Set aside.
2. Pre-heat the oven to 450 degrees F.
3. Clean the mushrooms by brushing away any visible dirt. If using shiitakes, remove the stem and slice the caps into 1/2 inch thick slices. If using maitakes, cut away about 2-3 inches of the base and break apart the mushroom into small, manageable chunks.
4. In a mixing bowl, toss the mushrooms with the sesame oil, salt and pepper.
5. Place the mushrooms on a roasting tray and bake for 8-10 minutes or until they have wilted and browned. Set aside.
6. Divide the chopped greens and pre-blanched noodles evenly into 6 large soup bowls.
7. Bring the Pho broth to a boil and then pour equal amounts over the noodles.
8. Garnish each bowl with the roasted mushrooms, evenly divided.
9. On a side plate, arrange the bean sprouts, scallions, cilantro and a small ramekin of Sriracha. Or, arrange all of the garnish ingredients except the Sriracha on top of the Pho, and place the Sriracha on the side.
10. Serve immediately.

Loving Hut Cities

Milpitas~California Palo Alto,~California San Francisco~California

Sacramento~California Alhambra~California San Diego~California

Elk Grove~California Claremont~California

Orange County~California San Jose ~ California
Upland~California Brea~California Fresno~California

Huntington Beach ~ California Orange ~ California Glendale ~ Arizona

Chicago ~ Illinois Cape Coral ~ Florida

New York City

Seattle~Washington New Jersey Naples~Florida

Worcester~Massachusetts Tampa~Florida

Cincinnati~Ohio Phoenix ~ Arizona Matawa ~ New Jersey Pittsburgh~
Pennsylvania Arlington ~ Texas Honolulu ~ Hawaii

Columbus~Ohio Falls Church~Virgina Portland~
Oregon Addison, Texas Toronto, Ontario Orlando, Florida

Norcross, Georgia Kennesaw, Georgia Houston, Texas

Loving Hut

Loving Hut is one of the largest families of vegan restaurants in the world. The chain has won numerous awards including *VegNews'* 2010 Favorite Vegan Restaurant award and the 2012 Vegan of The Year Award as seen on VegansAreCool.com. With more than 200 outlets in major cities all over the world, Loving Hut is the fastest growing vegan restaurant globally.

Loving Hut is a company that I hold close to my heart because of its spread of great vegan food around the globe, its noble intentions and its peaceful business practices. Loving Hut was created with a vision of living in peace and harmony with the earth and all beings. Each location provides delicious, high quality food at good value and convenience. Some recipes are served at a variety of locations; yet, most of the recipes are individual to each location.

A Note from Living Hut: "In essence, Loving Hut is to be a Loving House of Heaven, filled with divine light and warmth, where nourishing, Loving food for the body, mind, heart & spirit is served."

Loving Hut, Pittsburgh

Loving Hut Pittsburgh is a bright causal restaurant that serves exceptionally tasty Asian food with some Western options. They have a large menu containing many Loving Hut classics and mock meat dishes like the Jumbo Drumsticks, that are filled with soy ham, king mushrooms and served with the chef's perfect and light ginger sauce. You can experience the restaurant's delightful food yourself with the light and tasty Summer Roll recipe. The BBQ Noodle recipe makes an exceptional dish that is full of the bright flavors Loving Hut Pittsburgh is known for. Bite by bite you can fall in love with Loving Hut in Pittsburgh and Loving Huts around the globe!

BBQ Noodles

Loving Hut Pittsburgh

Preparation time: 30 minutes ~ Serves: 1 ~ Level of difficulty: 3

This is a delicious Asian style meal. The noodles and patties are oh, so yummy! When mixed with fresh veggies the recipes is lightened, and the sweet and sour marinade gives it a burst of flavor. It's fairly quick and easy to make and enjoyable to eat so give it a whirl!

Tip: The sweet and sour marinade is delicious but strongly flavoured so start with using just a little so you don't over power your dish.

Ingredients

2 tablespoons apple cider vinegar
4 tablespoons fresh lime juice
1 teaspoon soy sauce
1 tablespoons agave nectar
1 pinch of garlic, minced
2 tablespoons carrot, shredded
2 cups vermicelli rice noodles
two vegan crispy "egg" rolls

6 tablespoons vegan BBQ sauce, tamari or any thick brown vegan sauce
1/2 cup lettuce, shredded
several mint leaves, chopped for garnish
1/4 cup cucumber, chopped for garnish
1/3 cuo bean sprouts
2 Soy Delight protein patties (or seitan)
2 tablespoons peanuts, toasted, for garnish

Method

1. Combine the first six ingredients in a medium sauce dish and set aside to marinate.
2. Bring a medium pot of water to a boil and add vermicelli rice noodles. Boil for about 1-2 minutes or until the rice noodles are cooked but still firm. Immediately strain the rice noodles and run under cold water.
3. Bake the two crispy rolls in an oven at 350 degrees F for about 8 minutes or until heated all the way through.
4. In a pan over medium heat, add 4 tablespoons of the BBQ sauce and the rice noodles, evenly coating the noodles in the sauce. Transfer this mixture to a serving bowl so that the rice noodles are on one half of the bowl.
5. Add the lettuce, mint leaves, cucumber and bean sprouts to the other half of the bowl.
6. In the same pan, add 2 tablespoons of the BBQ sauce and the seitan or protein patties. Cook until heated through and each side has been immersed in the sauce. Arrange these on top of the noodles.
7. After the two crispy rolls are finished baking, cut each roll in half and place onto the rice noodles.
8. Garnish the bowl with toasted peanuts and accompany with the sweet and sour marinade.

Summer Rolls

Loving Hut Pittsburgh

Preparation time: 30 minutes ~ Serves: 2 ~ Level of difficulty: 2.5 ~ G/F

I love summer rolls. They are light and fresh. There are two Summer Roll recipes in Best Vegan. This one is simpler to make. The rolls' flavor is brightened by the basil and delightful dip.

Ingredients

For the Summer Rolls:
1 container of chicken flavoured Soy Delight (or any vegan textured soy protein that is chicken flavoured)
oil for frying, optional
1/2 cup or 1 carrot, peeled
1 small jicama, peeled
vegan margarine for frying
1 package of rice paper
2 large romaine lettuce leaves
2-8 fresh basil leaves

For the Peanut Sauce:
1/4 cup hoisin sauce
2 tablespoons peanut butter
small handful of toasted peanuts

Method

For the Summer Rolls:
1. Cut the soy protein into thin, rectangular, 4 inch long pieces.
2. Lightly pan-fry the soy protein in your preferred oil until all four sides are golden. Set aside to cool.
3. Grate the carrot.
4. Peel the jicama. Cut 8 long, thin 4 inch strips from the jicama.
5. Using the same pan, add a little vegan margarine and add the carrots and jicama. Cook until slightly softened but still crunchy, about 1-2 minutes on a high-medium heat. Allow the mixture to cool.
6. Fill a large bowl with hot water. Dip two sheets of rice paper, one at a time, into the water and place on a flat surface side by side. Make sure they are not touching one another.
7. Cut one romaine lettuce leaf in half and place each half at the bottom of each rice paper.
8. On each rice paper, place half the carrot mixture, 4 of pieces of jicama, half the soy protein mixture, and a couple of basil leaves.
9. Carefully roll the rice paper, folding in the sides half way through. Cut the two wraps into five pieces each and arrange on a small plate.

For the Peanut Sauce:
1. In a blender or using a whisk, mix hoisin sauce with peanut butter.
2. Put this mixture in a sauce dish and top with toasted peanuts to go along with the rolls.

Woodlands
Indian Vegetarian Cuisine

Woodlands Indian Vegetarian Cuisine opened in 2004 and has been recognized by media and guests as one of the best Indian restaurants in the state. It is a vegetarian restaurant that is largely vegan and appeals to many carnivores because of its exceptional food.

When walking into the restaurant one is comforted by a casual, homey feel and enticed by the delightful smells of South Indian food.

At lunch time the restaurant offers an exceptional buffet where each item is carefully crafted. There is also a full menu to order from with a surprisingly large variety of dinner entrées to try. Woodlands gifted Best Vegan with a delicious Samosa recipe. When golden brown and hot out of the oven these Samosas are the best around and flaunt the satisfying, ethnic flavors of the restaurant.

The Woodlands Story:

Woodlands Indian Vegetarian Cuisine has a triumphant story behind its success. The co-owner and chef Santosh Kotian found Woodlands' current physical location online, in the city Nashville, a place he had never been. There had been restaurants in that location previously, but they had not succeeded. Thus, in a city Santosh had never been to, in a location where restaurants had not survived, and as a new business owner, Santosh started Woodlands on a leap of faith.

With that faith he brought great knowledge of Indian food from his home land of South India. Woodlands was able to fill a niche and did it well with a large variety of incredible vegetarian food. Woodlands has a loyal following of people who were originally from India as well as people raised in Nashville.

Great spicing, variety, authenticity and quality has made Woodlands Indian Vegetarian Cuisine a joy and a success. I look forward to returning to Woodlands and biting into the heavenly flavors of Indian in Nashville.

Samosas
Woodlands Indian Vegetarian Cuisine

Preparation time: 1 hour ~ Level of difficulty: 4.5

Equipment: Kadhai, a thick, circular, deep cooking pot used in Indian cooking, Muslin cloth or another loose knit cotton cloth ~ S/F

These Samosas are crunchy and soft, filling and warm, combining classic potatoes, peas and carrots with a little Indian twist. Samosas are not the easiest things in the world to make. They take time but are heaps of fun, not costly and when hot out of the oven these are the best ones!

Ingredients

For the Samosa Pastry:
2 cups maida, fine all-purpose flour used in Indian cooking, or substitute with all-purpose or wheat flour
water to knead dough
2 tablespoons oil
1 pinch of salt
1/2 teaspoon cumin seeds
1/2 teaspoon Ajwain, spice found in Indian markets (optional)

For the Filling:
5-6 potatoes, boiled, peeled and mashed
3/4 cup each green peas and small cut carrots, boiled
1-2 green chilies, finely chopped (optional)
1 teaspoon cumin seeds
1/2 teaspoon ginger/garlic paste
1/2 teaspoon turmeric powder
red chili powder to taste
1/2 teaspoon garam masala
salt to taste
4 teaspoons oil
1/4 cup cilantro (or to taste), chopped

Serve with tomato ketchup, mint chutney, tamarind chutney or your own favorite.

Method

For the Samosa Pastry:
1. Mix flour, oil, cumin and ajwain with salt and water to make dough that is soft and elastic.
2. Cover the dough with moist muslin cloth—a loosely woven cotton cloth—and keep it aside for 20 minutes.

For the Filling:
1. Heat oil on medium heat in a non-stick pan. Fry all the ingredients, except the mashed potatoes and cilantro, for about 5 minutes.
2. Mix the fried ingredients with the mashed potatoes and cilantro. Set aside.

Assembly

1. Make small balls of dough and roll each into a 4 or 5 inch diameter circle. Cut each circle into two semi-circles.
2. Take one semi-circle and fold it into a cone shape. Use water to seal the edge.
3. Place a large spoonful of filling into the cone and seal the third side using a drop of water. Repeat for the rest of the samosas.
4. Heat the oil on medium in the kadhai. Deep fry until golden brown.
5. Serve with tomato ketchup, mint chutney and/or tamarind chutney.

Texas allures one with its sweet, charismatic people.

I have had some amazing vegan food in Dallas, Texas a city that was previously not known for its vegan cuisine.

served with southern charm and full of flavor.
Dallas Texas has great things to offer vegans.

Kalachandji's

A touch of India can be found in Dallas, Texas at Kalachandji's. The restaurant is Dallas's oldest vegetarian restaurant and is operated by the Hare Krishna Temple. This is a quietly spiritual place where the beautiful palace setting makes one feel as though they are being transported through time into a different culture. The Indian food is served buffet style and there is no set price, just a recommended donation. The sumptuous spread is prepared from recipes found in Vedic literatures dating back 5,000 years that use Ayurveda cooking principles, designed for the mind, body and spirit.

These recipes combine unique spicing and healthful, natural ingredients, resulting in light, flavorful and exotic dishes. Kalachandji's delicious food, beautiful atmosphere and enchanting traditions make the restaurant an unforgettable experience.

Kalachandji's is an oasis where you enter into the mood of ancient traditions, eat spicy, sweet, healthful Indian food, inhale exotic aromas and are immersed into a legend.

"One of the 100 best restaurants in Dallas."
D Magazine

"Best Vegetarian Restaurant"
WFAA-tv

"Best Vegetarian Restaurant"

"Among the South's Best Cheap Eats"

"Best Vegetarian Restaurant"
The Observer, Best of Dallas

"Excellent food."
Zagat Survey

"Best Healthy Dining"
AOL Cityguide

Kofta Balls in Tomato Sauce
Kalachandji's

Preparation time: 45 minutes ~ Serves: 4 ~ Level of difficulty: 3 ~ G/F & S/F

This is one of my favorite Indian meals. All the recipes from Kalachandji's are suburb and this dish follows the trend with its healthy ingredients and bright spicing. The ginger is a key component to the tomato sauce—its bold flavor smartly complements the lovely texture and gentle flavor of the Kofta Balls.

Ingredients

For the Kofta Balls:
2 cups cauliflower, grated
1 cup zucchini, grated
2 cups cabbage, grated
1 1/2 cups chickpea flour
1 teaspoon salt
1/2 teaspoon asafoetida powder (found at
Indian groceries)
1 teaspoon garam masala (found at Indian groceries)
2 teaspoons coriander, powdered
1/4 teaspoon turmeric
1 teaspoon ginger, minced
1 teaspoon jalapeño, minced
1/2 teaspoon baking powder
oil for deep-frying
salt to taste

For the Tomato Sauce:
2-3 tablespoons coconut oil
2 cinnamon sticks
1 teaspoon mustard seeds
3-4 curry leaves
1/2 teaspoon asafoetida powder
6-8 cups tomato puree
1 tablespoon tomato paste
[salt goes here]
2 teaspoons ginger, minced
1/2 teaspoon chili powder
1/2 teaspoon turmeric
1 teaspoon garam masala
2-3 teaspoons sugar
1/4 cup cilantro, chopped, for garnish

Method

For the Kofta Balls:
1. In a large mixing bowl, combine kofta ingredients and shape into 20-25 small balls.
2. Deep-fry over medium heat until golden brown. Drain.

For the Tomato Sauce:
1. Heat the coconut oil and add the cinnamon sticks and mustard seeds.
2. When the mustard seeds begin to crackle, add the curry leaves and asafoetida. Then add the tomato puree, tomato paste, salt, ginger, chili powder, turmeric, garam masala and sugar, and simmer for 10-12 minutes.
3. Add Kofta Balls and continue to simmer on low heat for 15-20 minutes.
4. Garnish with cilantro and serve hot.

Lemon Rice
Kalachandji's

Preparation time: 45 minutes ~ Serves: 4-6 ~ Level of difficulty: 3 ~ Equipment: Wok or deep frying pan ~ G/F

Lemon Rice is fantastic. The spices, cashews, raisins and lemon combine wonderfully resulting in a tangy and attractive dish. It's fairly simple to throw together, yet I feel like a skilled Indian chef while making it.

Ingredients

2 cups basmati or jasmine rice
6 tablespoons coconut oil
1 teaspoon mustard seeds
3 teaspoons channa dal (yellow lentils available in Indian markets)
1/2 cup cashews
1/4 cup raisins
1 teaspoon jalapeño, minced

1 teaspoon ginger, minced
3 or 4 curry leaves
1/4 teaspoon asafoetida powder (found at Indian groceries)
1/2 teaspoon turmeric
1/3 cup lemon juice, or juice from 2 to 3 fresh lemons
1/2 cup cilantro, finely chopped
salt to taste
1/4 cup coconut, grated for garnish

Method

1. Prepare rice in excess water like pasta, drain and keep aside.
2. Heat coconut oil in the wok and add mustard seeds.
3. When the mustard seeds begin to crackle, add the channa dal, cashews and raisins. Sauté for 3 to 5 minutes until dal and cashews are golden brown.
4. Add jalapeño, ginger, curry leaves, asafoetida and turmeric. Mix well.
5. Add rice, lemon juice, cilantro and salt. Mix well and cook for 5 minutes.
6. Garnish with coconut and serve hot.

Split Pea Dal Wada

Kalachandji's

In Advance: Soak split peas for 8 hours ~ Preparation time: 30 minutes ~ Serves: 4 ~ Level of difficulty: 2.5 ~ Equipment: Blender or Food processor~ G.F.

This is a high protein appetizer that is wonderfully spiced and deliciously fried. If you have all the spices it's simple and inexpensive to create.

Ingredients

2 cups yellow split peas, pre-soaked
2 tablespoons fresh ginger, minced
1 tablespoon jalapeño, minced
1/2 teaspoon asafoetida powder
(found and Indian groceries)
1/4 teaspoon turmeric

1 tablespoon curry leaves, chopped
1/4 teaspoon baking powder
11/2 teaspoons fennel seeds
1/4 cup cabbage, finely chopped
salt to taste
chutney to serve with

Method

1. Grind pre-soaked split peas in a blender or food processor until they reach a medium-fine paste.
2. Mix with all remaining ingredients in a large bowl.
3. Make small patties and fry over medium heat until golden brown.
4. Serve hot with chutney.

Mixed Vegetable Kurma
Kalachandji's

Preparation time: 25 minutes ~ Serves: 2 ~ Level of difficulty: 2.5 ~ Equipment: Wok or deep frying pan ~ G/F & S/F

This is one of the best ways to eat your veggies. It's easy to make and a great dish to try out if you are new to Indian cooking. Very similar to a mild curry, Kurma has a creamy sauce that's a little sweet and a little spicy and a lot delicious.

Ingredients

2 tablespoons coconut oil
2 cardamom pods
2 cloves
2 small cinnamon sticks
1 cup cabbage, finely shredded
2 cups coconut milk

1 teaspoon curry powder
3 cups mixed veggies of your choice, steamed
1 jalapeño, finely chopped
1 teaspoon cornstarch
salt to taste

Method

1. Heat coconut oil in a wok over medium heat.
2. Add cardamom, cloves and cinnamon sticks.
4. After the spices crackle, add the cabbage. Stir-fry over high heat until caramelized.
5. Add coconut milk, curry powder, steamed vegetables, jalapeño, cornstarch and salt. Cook for approximately 2-3 minutes and serve hot.

Yellow Mung Dal Soup

Kalachandji's Restaurant

Preparation time: 30 minutes ~ Serves: 4 ~ Level of difficulty: 2.5 ~ G/F & S/F

This is one of the most delicious soups I have ever tasted. It's flavored beautifully and is a bit of spicy India made to perfection. The yellow mung dal loses its form when cooked, forming the base of this bright, creamy soup. When preparing this healthy, high-protein, light soup you truly feel like a fantastic Indian cook.

Ingredients

1 cup yellow mung dal (found at Indian groceries)
1/3 teaspoon turmeric
1 1/2 teaspoons salt
6-8 cups water
2 teaspoons ginger, minced
1 teaspoon jalapeño, minced
2 teaspoons coriander, powdered
1 1/2 teaspoons cumin seeds, divided
2 zucchinis, cubed

2 tablespoons coconut oil
1/2 teaspoon mustard seeds
1 teaspoon asafoetida powder (found at Indian groceries)
3-4 curry leaves
2-3 tablespoons cilantro, finely chopped
lemon juice to taste

garnish with lemon wedges and serve over basmati or jasmine rice.

Method

1. Wash dal and drain.
2. In pot combine dal, turmeric, salt and water. Bring to a boil and simmer until half cooked. Remove the foam as it accumulates on top.
3. Add ginger, jalapeño, coriander powder, 1 teaspoon of the cumin seeds and zucchini. Continue simmering, stirring occasionally to keep the mixture from sticking to the bottom.
4. When the dal is soft, whisk to a smooth consistency.
5. Heat the coconut oil in a small saucepan. Add the mustard seeds and remaining cumin seeds.
6. When the seeds crackle add the asafoetida and curry leaves, and add to the dal mixture.
7. Stir well and garnish with cilantro. Add lemon juice to taste.
8. Serve hot with lemon wedges and rice.

You must be the change you
wish to see in the world.

Mahatma Gandhi

"You've gotta dance like there's nobody watching,
Love like you'll never be hurt,
sing like there's
nobody listening,
And live like it's heaven on earth."

William W. Purkey

Spiral Diner
And Bakery

Spiral Diner & Bakery has locations in Fort Worth and Dallas, Texas. Both places are simple, friendly and unpretentious with an uncanny knack for serving exceptionally delicious, vegan comfort food. The food is so exquisite that this casual vegan restaurant in middle of Cowtown, TX was awarded Best Vegetarian Restaurant in America by *VegNews Magazine*.

Restaurant owner Amy McNutt became a vegan overnight when she was involved in a film about factory-farmed cows in California and learned of the horrors of dairy and egg industry practices. She began to search for great vegan recipes. As she started mastering her art of making exceptional vegan food she started to dream about a restaurant of her own. In a attempt to provide vegan food to those she thought needed it most, she moved back to her Texas homeland and opened Spiral Diner & Bakery in August, 2002.

The restaurant was a quick success and its small location was bursting at the seams with customers. She moved Spiral Diner & Bakery to a larger location and opened a second branch several years later.

Some of the popularity of the place can be attributed to its inexpensive prices, organic ingredients and good-sized portions. The restaurants entice a variety of patrons, young and old, vegan and carnivore.

You can taste for yourself why such a large variety of people eat up the Spiral Diner & Bakery. The restaurant has included its recipe for Lone Star Vegan Chili—some of the tastiest chili I have found. It demonstrates what the restaurant is known for: classic comfort foods made exceptionally well. The Ranch Dressing recipe is also top notch. It is similar to classic ranch dressing but tastier, healthier and fresher.

The restaurant's menu includes a variety of organic beers and wines, fresh juices and organic smoothies. It has many options for appetizers and mains with lots of classic comfort food options like burgers and nachos and a variety of classic Mexican dishes. It also has great treats and baked goods, including one of the best cupcakes I have ever bitten into.

Spiral Diner & Bakery is a fun, friendly and consistently delicious place that brings a vegan spark to an area known as Cowtown. This vegan spark keeps getting stronger as a result of Spiral Diner & Bakery's great food and exceptional reputation.

Lone Star Vegan Chili

Spiral Diner & Bakery

Preparation time: 30 minutes ~ Serves: 4-6 ~ Level of difficulty: 2

This chili is special. It's far superior to other chilies and it is not expensive so you can make a massive batch, throw some in the freezer and have almost never-ending chili madness. It's a good low-budget, staple dish or a feed the masses meal.

Ingredients

2 tablespoons vegetable oil
1 white or onion, chopped
5 cloves garlic, chopped
1 28 ounce can crushed tomatoes
1 1/2 cups textured vegetable protein (TVP)
3-4 cups water
2 tablespoons chipotle puree

2 tablespoons chili powder
2 tablespoons cumin
1 1/2 teaspoon sea salt
1 tablespoons oregano
2 teaspoons vegetable broth powder
1 15 ounce can black beans
1 15 ounce can red kidney beans
vegan sour cream and chives for garnish

Method

1. In a large soup pot heat the vegetable oil over medium-high heat.
2. Add the onion and garlic and sautée until soft and translucent.
3. Stir in the rest of the ingredients and bring to a boil.
4. Simmer for about 10 minutes, adding more water if necessary.
5. Top with vegan sour cream and chives.

Ranch Dressing
Spiral Diner & Bakery

Preparation time: 10 minutes ~ Level of difficulty: 1 ~ Equipment: Blender or Food processor ~ G/F

This is the best ranch dressing I have ever had. It resembles classic ranch, yet tastes fresher with more exciting flavors. I mix it with some chopped cucumbers, tomatoes and carrots slices, throw on some fresh herbs and greens, and make a creamy vegan bowl of delight! This also makes a wonderful veggie dip.

Ingredients

1/2 cup Nayonaise or other vegan mayonnaise
1/2 cup Veganaise or other vegan mayonnaise
1/4 cup soymilk
1/2 teaspoon garlic salt
1/2 teaspoon garlic powder

1/2 teaspoon onion powder
1/4 teaspoon black pepper
2 rounded teaspoon fresh parsley, chopped
1 1/2 teaspoon apple cider vinegar
1/4 teaspoon dill

Method

1. Add all ingredients to the blender or food processor and blend until creamy.

900 South 234 West Salt Lake City, UT
sagescafe.com 801-322-3790

Sage's Cafe

"Best Vegetarian Restarant"   2002-2012
Salt Lake City Weekly Readers Choice Award

"Best Vegan Foods"
Salt Lake CityWeekly Readers Choice Award

"Most Fabulous Vegetarian Restaurant"
Q Salt Lake Magazine

"Top 20 Vegetarian Restaurants for Everyday Dining"
VegNews Magazine

"Top 50 Breakfast Spots in Utah"
Salt Lake Magazine

"Best Vegetarian Chef, Restaurateur"
VegNews Magazine

Chef Ian Brandt

Chef Ian Brandt opened Sage's Cafe in 1999, a place where his talent and creativity is tasted through his award-winning menu. He offers a selection of cuisine styles from across the globe.

The food is served in a welcoming and attractive restaurant. The restaurant includes a lovely cocktail lounge and seats 120 people. The great success of Sage's Cafe has led Ian Brandt to open two other vegan restaurants in Salt Lake City, The Vertical Diner and Café Super Natural, as well as a food supply company, Cali's Natural Foods.

He explains that the key to his success has been that he followed his passion and intuition. Ian encourages others to never give up.

" *love is the most important ingredient in anything in life*"

Chef Ian Brandt

219

Mushroom Stroganoff
Sage's Cafe

Preparation time: 30 minutes ~ Serves: 4 ~ Level of difficulty: 3 ~ G/F

Unbelievable! This Mushroom Stroganoff does not taste like a vegan dish, as it has a fantastic creamy white sauce. Its perfectly seasoned with a hint of sherry and chunks of portabella mushroom bringing it a flavorful heartiness. I make it with brown rice linguine noodles, which are healthy and make the dish gluten-free.

Ingredients

1 tablespoon sesame oil
1 tablespoon olive oil
1/2 teaspoon dry thyme leaf or 2 teaspoons fresh thyme leaf
1/2 teaspoon dry rubbed sage leaf or 2 teaspoons of fresh sage leaf
1/2 teaspoon dry French tarragon or 2 teaspoons of fresh tarragon leaf
pinch white pepper
5 cranks fresh ground black pepper
pinch cayenne
pinch sea salt

2 portabella caps, diced
2 cloves garlic, minced
1/4 cup sherry
1 tablespoon tamari
3/4 cup soup stock or water
2 cups dairy-free sour cream
12 ounces of pasta
burgundy wine reduction syrup, minced fresh sage, fresh ground black pepper or dairy-free cheese for garnish

Method

1. Sautée onions, bell peppers, oil, herbs and diced portabellas over medium heat. If using fresh herbs, add these at the end of the sautée.
2. When onion is almost translucent add minced garlic and lower heat.
3. When garlic, onions and peppers are completely cooked deglaze (remove food partials from pan) with sherry and tamari.
4. Add the dairy-free sour cream. Adjust consistency with stock or water as needed. The sauce should be the consistency of marinara sauce.
5. Boil pasta as required on package.
6. Toss cooked pasta with the stroganoff sauce
7. Garnish with burgundy wine reduction syrup, minced fresh sage, fresh ground black pepper or vegan parmesan cheese.

Picadillo Vegetarian
Sage's Cafe

Preparation time: 45 minutes ~ Serves: 4 ~ Level of difficulty: 3 ~ G/F

This is one of those very special recipes that is exceptionally healthy, light and wonderfully delicious! It can also be used as a base for many other preparations such as burritos and tacos, or can be served as a side dish. The spices and ingredients combine marvellously into a beautifully flavored dish.

Ingredients

3 tablespoons olive oil
1 cup black beans, cooked or canned
1/2 cup baked* tofu, diced
2 cup brown rice, cooked
1 cup vegetables of choice, chopped
1 teaspoon salt
1 teaspoon chilli powder
1 teaspoon nutmeg

1 teaspoon cumin
1 teaspoon paprika
1/4 teaspoon cayenne
1/2 tablespoon garlic, minced
1/4 cup cilantro, chopped
1/2 cup tomato, diced
avocado, cilantro sprigs, black olives, capers, pickles and oven roasted table grapes for garnish

* To bake tofu, place on a sheet pan in the oven set to 375 degrees F for 30 minutes, turning once.

Method

1. In a large pan, heat olive oil to medium and add black beans, tofu, brown rice, vegetables, salt, chilli powder, nutmeg, cumin, paprika and cayenne. Simmer for 10 minutes or until all ingredients are thoroughly cooked.
2. Mix in garlic, cilantro and tomato.
3. Place in serving dish and top with avocado, cilantro sprig, black olives, capers, pickles and oven roasted table grapes.

Raw Fresh Herb Cashew Pate

Sage's Cafe

In Advance: Soak cashews for 6 hours ~ Preparation time: 10 minutes ~ Yields: 3 cups ~ Level of difficulty: 1 ~ Equipment: Blender ~ G/F & S/F

This raw pate is quick and easy to make. It reminds me of a light, fluffy cream cheese. You can taste a hint of lemon, mixed with the chosen herb. It's a versatile item and I like to have it around all the time so I can enjoy it on appropriate dishes. I am a little hooked! It is also served as part of a raw foods plate with raw vegetables, raw crackers, lettuce leaves and/or vegetable noodles. Serve as a cracker topper for an appetizer, or as a sandwich or wrap spread with some fresh avocado.

Ingredients

4 cups raw cashews, soaked and drained
1 cup water
3 tablespoons fresh pressed lemon juice
1 teaspoon salt

1/4 teaspoon fine ground white pepper
2 teaspoons rosemary or 2 tablespoons chives or oregano, minced

Method

1. Put all ingredients except the herbs in a blender, and blend until creamy.
2. Add the herbs and blend for 15 seconds.

222

Seattle, Washington

Seattle, the great wealthy city that pours rain through the winter then blasts sunshine for perfect summer weather. The city boasts beautiful water and mountain views.

I like to wander the markets, visit the Space Needle and most of all, eat the city's fabulous food.
Capitol Hill is famous for its vegan options and across the city, Cafe Flora tempts foodies with the tastiest delights. Seattle's beauty, wonderful summers and great food make it exceptional

Cafe Flora Chef Janine Doran

Cafe Flora Owner Nat Stratton-Clarke

Cafe Flora

Cafe Flora has a friendly vibe and a hip, attractive atmosphere. When entering one can see a breath-taking atruim to the right, flaunting garden-style café tables and chairs, a large skylight, greenery, slate floors and a bubbling stone fountain. Inside, the walls are brightened with uplifting artwork and natural greenery.

The dishes excel in flavor and creativity with global influence and seasonal changes.

When eating in Cafe Flora each delicious bite is a demonstration of why the restaurant is known as Seattle's most exceptional vegetarian restaurant.

It's ethical, hip and completely cravable.

honorable mentions

Best Vegetarian Restaurant 2013
Seattle Magazine

Best Salad 2013
Seattle Magazine

Best Vegetarian Food 2013
Citysearch Seattle

People's Choice Awards – Best Green Restaurant Seattle 2012
Nature's Plate

Best Vegetarian in Seattle
Local Eats

Top 100 Restaurants
Local Eats

Peoples Pic Favorite Local Vegetarian
nwsource.com

Best Vegetarian Restaurants in the U.S.
Travel + Leisure Magazine

Hoppin' John Fritters

with Cayenne Aioli
Cafe Flora

In Advance: Cook black-eyed peas if you do not use canned ones ~ Preparation: 40 minutes plus 30 minutes to chill ~ Level of difficulty: 3 ~ Serves: 6 ~ Equipment: Food processor or Blender ~ G/F

Hoppin' John Fritters are a flavor delight—crispy on the outside, warm on the inside and packed with fresh herb flavors. The slightly spicy dollops of creamy Cayenne Aioli make this delicious appetizer. They are fairly easy and inexpensive to make and are packed with protein.

Ingredients

For the Fritters:
2 cups dried black-eyed peas, soaked for 2-8 hours or 4 (14.5-ounce) cans
1 tablespoons olive oil
1 large carrot, peeled and finely diced
2 stalks celery, finely diced
1 small red onion, finely diced
1 tablespoon chopped fresh sage, or 1 teaspoon dried
1 teaspoon minced garlic
1/4 cup white wine
1 cup cooked white rice, cooled

3 tablespoons fresh Italian parsley, chopped
2 to 3 sprigs thyme, leaves picked
1/2 bunch whole scallions, chopped
1 smoked chipotle chile in adobo, minced
1 teaspoon salt

1 tablespoon cornstarch
vegetable oil for frying

For the Vegan Mayonnaise:
1 12 ounce package silken tofu
2 tablespoons fresh squeezed lemon juice
2 teaspoons salt
3 tablespoons Dijon mustard
1/2 cup canola oil

For the Cayenne Aioli:
1/2 cup Vegan Mayonnaise
2 teaspoons fresh squeezed lemon juice
1/4 teaspoon cayenne pepper
2 teaspoons Dijon mustard
2 cloves garlic, minced

Method

For the Fritters:
1. Drain pre-soaked black-eyed peas and place them in a pot, covered with about an inch of water. Bring to a boil, lower the heat and simmer uncovered until tender, 45-60 minutes. Add water as needed. Drain and set aside to cool. If you're using canned black-eyed peas, rinse them under cold water and drain.
2. Heat the olive oil in a skillet over medium heat. Add the carrot, celery, red onion and sage. Sauté until the onion is soft and translucent, about 10 minutes. Add the garlic and cook for 1 more minute. Add the wine and stir. Cook until all the wine has evaporated and the mixture is dry. Set aside to cool.
3. Reserve 2 cups of black-eyed peas. Put the remaining peas into the bowl of a mixer. With a paddle attachment, mash the peas until they begin to stick together (you can also do this by hand using a potato masher).
4. Add the vegetables, rice, herbs, scallions, chipotle chile, and salt to the bean mixture. Mix well.
5. Sprinkle cornstarch over the fritter mix and stir for 1 minute. Gently fold in the reserved peas, trying to keep some peas whole. Chill the mixture for half an hour before forming into patties.
6. Using 3 tablespoons of the mixture for each fritter, shape it into balls. Gently flatten each ball with your fingertips into a patty about 2 1/2 inches in diameter. Smooth out the jagged edges so they don't break off when you cook them. Lay the patties on an ungreased baking sheet.
7. Heat oil in a large heavy skillet over medium-high heat. Put several patties in the pan, leaving enough room to flip them easily. Cook on each side until browned and crisp, 4 to 5 minutes per side. Cook the remaining fritters in the same way.
8. Drain the fritters on paper towels, keeping them warm in a 200 degree F oven until ready to serve.
9. Serve 2 or 3 fritters with a dollop of Cayenne Aioli.

For the Cayenne Aioli:
1. In a food processor or blender, combine all Vegan Mayonnaise ingredients except the oil. Process until well blended. With the machine running, drizzle in the canola oil slowly until it is fully combined.
2. Whisk all Cayenne Aioli ingredients in a small bowl and refrigerate until ready to serve.

Lentil Pecan Pate
Cafe Flora

Preparation time: 35 minutes ~ Serves: 4 ~ Level of difficulty: 2.5 ~ Equipment: Food processor ~ G/F

This pate is very popular at Cafe Flora and with good reason. The flavor is exceptional—you can taste the slow-cooked onions, hints of miso and herbs. At Cafe Flora, it is served with crackers, olives and fruit, which makes an excellent appetizer or share plate.

Ingredients

1 cup red lentils
2 cups water
1 bay leaf
1 tablespoon olive oil
1 medium onion, diced
1 tablespoon garlic, chopped
1/2 teaspoon dried thyme
1/2 teaspoon dried sage

2 tablespoons mirin or sweet rice wine
1 teaspoon umeboshi (sour plum) paste
1 tablespoon light miso
1/2 cup pecan pieces, toasted
1/2 teaspoon salt
1/2 teaspoon freshly ground pepper

Method

1. Rinse the lentils. Put them in a pot with the water and bay leaf.
2. Bring to a boil over medium heat, lower the heat and simmer, covered, until the lentils are very soft and most of the water has been absorbed, about 15 to 20 minutes. Add more water if necessary. Remove the bay leaf, and set the lentils aside to cool.
3. While the lentils are cooking, heat the olive oil in a pan over medium heat. Add the onion and cook until it has reduced in volume and begun to soften, about 5 minutes. Stir once or twice.
4. Turn the heat to low, and cook the onion for an additional 15 to 20 minutes, stirring occasionally. If the onion starts to stick, add 1 or 2 tablespoons of water (or cooking sherry), and stir to remove any bits of onion from the bottom of the pan. When done, the onion should be various shades of brown, soft and sweet.
5. Add the garlic, thyme and sage to the onion and cook for 1 minute. Remove from the heat and set aside to cool.
6. Put the lentils and onion mixture in a food processor. Add all the remaining ingredients and process until the mixture is a smooth paste. Transfer to a bowl, cover and chill before serving. Serve with mixed olives, seasonal fresh fruit and crackers.

Monty's Blue Plate Diner

In 1990, Monty's Blue Plate Diner took over what was previously a gas station and opened its doors for service. Since then it has received a host of awards and created a great reputation.

The first priority when visiting Monty's Blue Plate Diner is soaking in the buzzing atmosphere, which has a hip, 1960s diner feeling. It's a great place to be. Inside it is bright blue and white with a bar to the back and booths scattered along the sides of the restaurant.

Monty's Blue Plate Diner is open all day serving breakfast and delicious vegan lunch and dinner options. Vegetarian and non-vegetarian food is served as well.

You can taste a bit of Monty's amazing breakfast for yourself with the Tempeh and Vegetable Hash recipe, which is a classic breakfast made vegan. It is a hearty breakfast, being full of veggies, potatoes and tempeh which is nicely seasoned and pan seared. The Lemon Tahini Spread recipe is full of garlic and lemon flavors, which enhance any dish. You can taste the spread in some of Monty's excellent sandwiches.

A main purpose and commitment for the restaurant is to support its community using as much local produce as possible. Monty's also aides a variety of Wisconsin-based charities and in Madison has created the most delicious parts of the community!

"A Place for Every Taste"
Food Fight Restaurant Group

"Best of Madison"
Madison Magazine

"Best Breakfast"
The Isthmus Newspaper

"Best Vegetarian Menu"
The Isthmus Newspaper

Lemon Tahini Spread
Monty's Blue Plate Diner

Preparation time: 10 minutes ~ Level of difficulty: 2 ~ G/F & S/F

This is a raw creamy spread that's got a lot of kick. Fresh garlic kick, that is! The garlic, lemon and tahini combine wonderfully. Monte's Blue Plate Diner recommends serving this spread on sandwiches or pita or using it as a salad dressing. The restaurant serves it on a sandwich with roasted mushrooms. Tahini paste is available in most supermarkets and in ethnic grocery stores in prepared or raw form. Either will make this spread a delicious success.

Ingredients

2 cups tahini paste
1 cup water
1 cup lemon juice, fresh squeezed
1/4 cup garlic, minced

1 teaspoon salt
6 green onions, thinly sliced
1 tablespoon sugar

Method

1. Combine all the ingredients in a bowl and mix well.

Tempeh and Vegetable Hash

Monty's Blue Plate Diner

Preparation time: 30 minutes ~ Serves: 4 ~ Level of difficulty: 3

This is a good old-fashioned breakfast, with a little new fashion flare, via tempeh. This meal is nicely seasoned, yet remains simple. Fried onions, potatoes and peppers classically complement one another and the marinated tempeh gives the dish a heartiness. It's an American home-style breakfast gone vegan!

Ingredients

For the Tempeh:
2 packages of tempeh, thinly sliced
1/4 cup soy sauce
1/4 cup olive oil

For the Vegetable Hash:
1 yellow onion, diced
1 red bell pepper, diced
1 green bell pepper, diced

4 cups red potatoes, medium dice, boiled
1 tablespoon fennel seed
1 tablespoon oregano
1/2 teaspoon red chili flake
1/2 tablespoon salt
1 teaspoon black pepper

Method

For the Marinated Tempeh:
1. Lay the tempeh on a baking sheet and drizzle with the soy sauce and olive oil.
2. Bake at 350 degrees F for 12-15 minutes.

For the Vegetable Hash:
1. Combine all of the ingredients in a large mixing bowl.
2. Dice the cooked tempeh and add to the mixture.
3. When ready to serve, sautée the hash in a little bit of canola or olive oil until the potatoes are nicely browned.

Burt Family Food Services

David Burt was co-founder and head chef at The Red Avocado, the exceptional vegan restaurant that served Iowa City from 1999 to 2012. During its time it was voted in the top ten vegetarian restaurants in the country by TripAdvisor and PETA. The Red Avocado was featured over the years in *The New York Times*, *USA Today*, *Bon Appetit*, *Midwest Living* and *Travel Savvy*.

The Red Avocado sadly came to a end in the beginning of 2013 as the building was demolished to make space for residential and commercial buildings. The former partner of The Red Avocado, Katy Meyer, moved on to open the vegan restaurant, Trumpet Blossom Café and David Burt started Burt Family Food Services.

Through his new business he continues to promote local, plant-based cuisine with weekly prepared meals, veggie burgers, vegan cooking classes and nutritional consultations. He also supplies several local restaurants with his products.

The Red Avocado no longer exists yet the recipes David Burt sent to me while it was open are exceptional and display David Burt's talents and abilities from his plate to yours. Enjoy the spices, the delightful flavors and the great nutrition in the Carrot Chipotle Pate and Saag Paneer.

Carrot Chipotle Pate

by David Burt

Preparation time: 20 minutes ~ Level of difficulty: 2 ~ Serves: 8 ~ Equipment: Food processor ~ G/F & S/F

Creamy, slightly sweet and with a touch of spice. Delightful! This pate goes over well with everyone and is a perfect appetizer at your dinner party. It's inexpensive, healthy and tasty!

Ingredients

3 pounds carrots, peeled, roughly chopped and steamed 10 minutes with 1-2 teaspoons salt
2 tablespoons fresh lemon juice
2 tablespoons paprika
3 tablespoons ground coriander

1 tablespoons chipotle powder or 1 teaspoon canned chipotles
3/4 cup sunflower oil
1 teaspoon salt
1 teaspoon brown sugar

Serve with pita bread

Method

1. Place all ingredients in food processor and blend until smooth.
2. Serve with warmed pita bread.

Saag Paneer
by David Burt

In Advance: Bake tofu, Cook spinach and Roast cumin ~ Preparation time: 30 min ~ Level of difficulty: 4 ~ Equipment: Food processor ~ Serves: 4 ~ G/F

I love Indian food! It's a joy to cook with exotic spices and create a masterpiece from across the ocean. Saag Paneer is a light dish with a creamy texture, pleasantly spiced with classic Indian spices that give it ample flavor without being over-whelming. This particular recipe is creates the best Saag Paneer I have had. I crave it regularly and keep it on cooking repeat.

Ingredients

For the Baked Tofu:
1 package firm tofu
1 tablespoon sunflower or vegetable oil
2 tablespoons tamari
2 tablespoons fresh lemon juice
1-2 cloves garlic, finely minced

For the Saag Paneer:
2 tablespoons sesame or vegetable oil
1 tablespoon cumin seed
1 teaspoon yellow mustard seed
1 teaspoon fennel seed
4 cups cooked, drained, spinach (frozen is fine, for cooking fresh, see below)
4 cups onion, diced

1 jalapeño or serrano pepper
2 cups leeks, diced
2 cups celery, diced
2-4 cloves garlic, minced
2-4 teaspoons ginger, grated
4 tablespoons vegetable stock
1 teaspoon coriander, ground
4 green onions, finely sliced
2-4 tablespoons fresh lemon juice
1 tablespoon roasted cumin, ground (see below)
salt and pepper to taste
1-3 slices baked tofu, diced

Method

For the Baked Tofu:
1. Pre-heat the oven to 350 degrees F.
2. Drain package of firm tofu and wrap in a thick rag or towel. Weigh it down to squeeze out excess water, pouring off and changing the towel if necessary. This takes about 30 minutes. If time is short, you can simply squeeze the block of tofu wrapped in a towel repeatedly but not so much that the tofu crumbles. Towel should be good and wet after you are done.
3. While the tofu is draining, whisk together the sunflower oil, tamari, lemon juice and garlic. Slice the pressed tofu into 3 slices and place on an oven pan. Pour the marinade over the tofu and let marinate for 30 minutes. The better drained the tofu, the more the marinade will infuse into it.
4. Bake for 12-18 minutes. The marinade should either be gone or sizzling well when the tofu is done. Refrigerate until ready to use.

Tip: If you eat a lot of tofu, a larger batch can be made and will keep (covered) for 3-5 days in the fridge. As you use more tofu per batch you will use proportionately less marinade per block of tofu. For six packages of tofu you would need about three times the amount of marinade.

For the Fresh Spinach:

1. Fill a large pot or bowl 3/4 full with cold water. Place spinach in the vessel until there is half spinach and half water. Gently push down the spinach into the water and let it rise again a few times. The dirt will sink.

2. Place the spinach into a colander and let drain. Repeat until no dirt remains.

3. The key here is to lift the spinach out of the water and not pour off the water through the spinach, which only remixes the dirt back into the spinach. After the last wash, drain in colander, but do not spin dry. Some water should remain clinging to the spinach leaves.

4. Drain a little at a time, placing the spinach in a wide pan or pot that has a tight-fitting lid. You will probably need at least 2 pounds of fresh spinach to make 4 cups cooked. Spinach has "lift" so push gently down to get all of it in the pot or pan.

5. Once all the spinach is washed, drained and in the pot, sprinkle a tablespoon of salt over it, place it on the stove on medium heat and cover. Check after 5 minutes. If not done, stir up, cover and check again after a minute or two. When done, all the spinach will have sunk and should still be tender and bright green. Drain it and squeeze gently to remove excess water.

For the Roasted Cumin:

1. Heat a heavy saucepan to medium-high heat. Add 1/4 cup whole cumin seeds and toss continuously in pan. Seeds will change color slightly and an intense aroma will come off. This should only take 10-30 seconds if your pan is hot. The key is noticing the aroma.

2. Before the seeds burn, pour them out of the pan onto a plate to cool. These whole seeds can be kept sealed for 1-3 months.

3. Grind them only before you are about to use them.

For the Saag Paneer:

1. Heat a pan on medium-high and add the oil. swirl, add the cumin, mustard and fennel seeds and let sizzle about 3-5 seconds.

2. Add the onions and sauté 1 minute.

3. Add the garlic, jalapeño or serrano, leek and celery, and sauté 2-3 more minutes.

4. Add the ginger.

5. Turn the heat down to medium and stir often. Sauté until onions are golden. Add stock and ground coriander.

6. Turn the heat up and bring to a boil. Add spinach and stir to mix. Cover, turn heat down to medium-low and cook for 5 minutes or so.

7. Blend in a food processor, adding lemon juice and ground roasted cumin as it blends.

8. When the sauce is smooth, return to the pan on low heat. Add baked tofu and cover until tofu has warmed through, about 3-5 minutes.

9. Serve topped with a dollop of soy butter.

Note: This can be more saucy or more "tofu-ey" depending on your taste. In spinach season, large batches can be made and frozen.

Chestnuts
Harvest Vegetable Platter, 55

Chick Peas
Butternut Squash Soup 96
Chick pea flour, Swedish Vegetable Cakes 128
Chick pea flour, Kofta Balls in Tomato Sauce 209
Pastrami Spiced Young Carrots 192
The Sufi Poet 100

Chillies
Grilled "Chicken" Mexican Mole 59
Jalapeno, Fiddlehead and Potato Curry 172
Jalapeno, Raw Curried Samosas 123
Jalapeno, Saag Paneer 237
Jalepeno, Lemon Rice 210
Jalepeno, Split Pea Dal Wada 212
Kofta Balls in Tomato Sauce 209
Raw Kelp Noodle Salad 165
Samosas 202
Spinach Mushroom Loaf 133
Tomato Basil Coulee 134
Yellow Mung Dal Soup 213

Chipotle
Carrot Chipotle Pate 236
Grilled "Chicken" Mexican Mole 59
Hoppin' John Fritters 227
Lone Star Vegan Chili 217
Roasted Kabocha Squash Salad, with Chipotle Dressing 37
Seitan Loaf 111

Chocolate
Brownies, 46
Chocolate Chip Cookies 76
Chocolate Ganache 169
Chocolate Ganache Filling 50
Chocolate Orange Mousse Pie 115
Chocolate Silk Pie Filling or Pudding 69
Chocolate Tart 50

Grilled "Chicken" Mexican Mole 59
Ice Cream Sandwiches 78
Taza Chocolate Cheesecake 109

Coconut
Raw Key Lime Pie 152

Coconut, milk
Butternut Squash Soup 96
Chocolate Orange Mousse Pie 115
Chocolate Silk Pie Filling or Pudding 69
Curry Apple Tofu 10
Mixed Vegetable Kurma 211
Pumpkin Spice French Toast 181
Spaghetti Squash Cakes 86
Strawberry Blonde Smoothie 24
Taza Chocolate Cheesecake 109
Thai Corn Cakes 187

Coconut, oil
Asian Long Bean and Tempeh Salad 36
Coconut Oil Pie Crust 68
Kofta Balls in Tomato Sauce 209
Lemon Rice 210
Macerated Summer Fruit Tart 70
Mixed Vegetable Kurma 211
Raw Key Lime Pie 152
Yellow Mung Dal Soup 213

Coconut, shredded
Asian Long Bean and Tempeh Salad 36
Raw Key Lime Pie 152
Raw Three Berry Pie 156
Yogi Wraps 21

Curry
Curry Apple Tofu 10
Fiddlehead and Potato Curry 172
Lemon Rice 210
Mixed Vegetable Kurma 211
Raw Curried Samosas 123
Split Pea Dal Wada 212
Yellow Mung Dal Soup 213

Daikon
Marinated Tofu Salad 67

Dates, medjool
Raw Key Lime Pie 152
Raw Pecan Sushi with Tempura 166
Raw Three Berry Pie 156
Raw Tortilla Soup 26

Fiddleheads
Fiddlehead and Potato Curry 172

Garam Masala
Fiddlehead and Potato Curry 172
Kofta Balls in Tomato Sauce 209
Raw Curried Samosas 123
Samosas 202

Gluten-free
Apple Mint Chutney 22
Apple Cranberry Sauce 55
Almond Sauce 145
Baked Tofu 237
Balsamic Vinaigrette 102
Braised Tofu with Quinoa 129
Butternut Squash Soup 96
Bloodroot Burger 62
Caramelized Brussels Sprouts 94
Carrot Chipotle Pate 236
Caper Soy Mayonnaise Sauce 86
Cashew Crème 180
Cayenne Aioli 228
Chermoula Oil 40
Chermoula Vinaigrette 40
Chocolate Ganache 169
"Chicken" Marinade 59
Chimmichurri Dipping Sauce 123
Coconut Curry Pate 22
Coconut Syrup 187
Curry Apple Tofu 10
Fiddlehead and Potato Curry 172

Gluten-free
Fried Brussel Sprouts 118
Green Smoothie 29
Grillin Glaze 44
Grilled 'Chicken' Mexican Mole 59
Hoppin' John Fritters 227
Kofta Balls in Tomato Sauce 209
Le Fricot 139
Lemon Tahini Dressing 186
Lemon Tahini Spread 233
Lentil Pecan Pate 230
Lemon Rice 210
Long Bean Salad 36
Marinated Baked Tofu Salad 173
Marinated Tofu Salad 67
Marinated Tofu 174
Mediano Rice and Pinto Beans 59
Mexican Mole 59
Mid-East Lentils and Rice 65
Minted Puree Dipping Sauce 123
Miso Glaze 166
Mixed Vegetable Kurma 212
Mushroom Pho 183
Mushroom Stroganoff 220
Mustard Sauce 128
Nut Meat 89
Pastrami Spiced Young Carrots 192
Pasta Salad Dressing 160
Peanut Sauce 200
Pho Broth 193
Picadillo Vegetarian 221
Pico Sauce 89
Quinoa Tabouli 149
Ranch Dressing 218
Raw Beanless Hummus 105
Raw Curried Samosas 123
Raw Fresh Herb Cashew Pate 222
Raw Kale Salad 90
Raw Kelp Noodle Salad 165
Raw Key Lime Pie 152
Raw Mock Tuna Salad 155
Raw Nori Wrap 106

Gluten-free
Raw Pecan Sushi with Tempura 166
Raw Pecan Pate 166
Raw Pie Crust 152 & 156
Raw Stuffed Avocado 89
Raw Three Berry Pie 156
Raw Tempura 166
Raw Tortilla Soup 26
Red Lentil Hummus 101
Red Rice and Fava Bean Salad 40
Roasted Garlic 136
Roasted Kabocha Squash Salad 37
Roasted Parsnips and Carrots 55
Rutabaga Potato Puree 55
Saag Paneer 237
Smokey Tomato Aioli 135
Sour Crème & Onion Kale Chips 30
Split Pea Dal Wada 211
Strawberry Blonde Smoothie 24
Stuffed Mushrooms 145
Summer Rolls 200
Super Grain Salad (without Fakin Bacon) 186
Swedish Vegetable Cakes 128
Thai Corn Cakes 187
The Sufi Poet 100
Tofu Marinade 67
Tomato and Cucumber Coulis Dipping Sauce 123
Tomato Basil Coulee 134
Tomato Delight 9
Tomato Sauce 209
Ume Plum Paste 51
Vegan Mayonnaise 228
Vegetable Hash 234
Wasabi Sauce 51
Wild Mushroom Tofu Scramble 180
Wild Raw Tomato Soup 19
Yellow Mung Dal Soup 213
Yogi Wraps 21

Hot sauce
Grillin' Glaze 44
Mushroom Pho 183

Ice Cream
Ice Cream Sandwiches 78

Indian
Fiddlehead and Potato Curry 172
Kofta Balls in Tomato Sauce 209
Lemon Rice 210
Mixed Vegetable Kurma 212
Raw Curried Samosas 123
Saag Paneer 237
Samosas 202
Sea Palm Strudel 51
Split Pea Dal Wada 211
Yellow Mung Dal Soup 213

Kale
Bloodroot Burger 62
Green Smoothie 29
Raw Kale Salad 90
Sour Crème & Onion Kale Chips 30
Swedish Vegetable Cakes 128

Lentils
Bloodroot Burger 62
Le Fricot 139
Lemon Rice 210
Lentil Pecan Pate 230
Mid-East Lentils and Rice 65
Red Lentil Hummus 101
The Sufi Poet 100

Liquid Smoke
Grillin' Glaze, 44
Smokey Tomato Aioli 135
Super Grain Salad with Fakin' Bacon and Lemon Tahini Dressing 185

Mexican
Grilled "Chicken" Mexican Mole 59
Lone Star Vegan Chilli 217
Picadillo Vegetarian 221

Middle East
Mid-East Lentils and Rice 65
Quinoa Tabouli 149
Red Lentil Hummus 101
Tabouli 160

Mushrooms
Mushroom Walnut Pate 64

Mushrooms, chanterelle
Pot Stickers 35
Spinach Mushroom Loaf 133
Tempeh Bourguignon 122
Wild Mushroom Tofu Scramble 180

Mushrooms, cremini
Fried Brussels Sprouts 118
Tempeh Bourguignon 122

Mushrooms, enoki
Raw Kelp Noodle Salad, 165

Mushrooms, French horn
Quinoa Tabouli 149

Mushrooms, maitake
Mushroom Pho 183

Mushrooms, portabella
Mushroom Pho 183
Mushroom Stroganoff 220
Tempeh Bourguignon 122

Mushroom, powder
Curry Apple Tofu 10
Stuffed Mushrooms 145
Tempeh Bourguignon 122
Tomato Delight 9

Mushrooms, shitake
Harvest Vegetable Platter, 55
Mushroom Pho 183
Stuffed Mushrooms 145
Tomato Delight 9
Yogi Wraps 21

Nettles
Wild Raw Tomato Soup 19

Noodles
BBQ Noodles 197
Mushroom Pho 183
Mushroom Stroganoff 220
Pasta Salad 160
Raw Kelp Noodle Salad, 165

Nutritional Yeast
Harvest Vegetable Platter, 55
Sour Crème & Onion Kale Chips 30
Wild Mushroom Tofu Scramble 180

Peanuts
BBQ Noodles 197
Grilled "Chicken" Mexican Mole 59
Summer Rolls 200
Vietnamese Summer Rolls 66

Pecans
Lentil Pecan Pate 230
Raw Pecan Sushi with Tempura 166
Raw Three Berry Pie 156

Phyllo Wrapping
Sea Palm Strudel 51

Pies
Banana Crème Pie 14
Chocolate Orange Mousse Pie 115
Chocolate Silk Pie Filling or Pudding 69
Macerated Summer Fruit Tart 70
Raw Key Lime Pie 152
Raw Three Berry Pie 156

Pine Nuts
Red Rice and Fava Bean Salad 39

Plums
Lentil Pecan Pate 230
Pasta Salad 160
Plum sauce 51

Pumpkin
Pumpkin Spic French Toast 181
Roasted Kabocha Squash Salad, with Pumpkin Brittle 37

Quinoa
Bloodroot Burger 62
Braised Tofu with Quinoa 129
Quinoa Tabouli 149
Super Grain Salad with Fakin' Bacon and
Lemon Tahini Dressing 185

Rice
Basmati, Bloodroot Burger 62
        Lemon Rice 210
Bhutanese red, Red Rice and Fava Bean
Salad 39
Brown, Spinach Mushroom Loaf 133
        Picadillo Vegetarian 221
Grano mediano, Grilled "Chicken" Mexican
Mole 59
Jasmine, Lemon Rice 210
White, Mid-East Lentils and Rice 65

Rolls
Summer Rolls 200
Vietnamese Summer Rolls 66

Sea Palm
Sea Palm Strudel 51

Seaweed
Marinated Baked Tofu Salad 173
Raw Kelp Noodle Salad 165
Raw Mock Tuna Salad 155
Raw Nori Wrap 106
Raw Pecan Sushi with Tempura 166
Spaghetti Squash Cakes 86

Seeds
Caraway, Swedish Vegetable Cakes 128
Hemp, Sour Crème & Onion Kale Chips 30
Pumpkin, Roasted Kabocha Squash Salad 37
Super Grain Salad with Fakin' Bacon and
Lemon Tahini Dressing 185
Sesame, Vietnamese Summer Rolls 66
        Raw Beanless Hummus 105
        Raw Nori Wrap 106
        Stuffed Mushrooms 145
        Sea Palm Strudel 51
Grilled "Chicken" Mexican Mole 59
Mushroom Walnut Pate 64
Oatmeal Sunflower Bread, 63
Sunflower, Harvest Vegetable Platter 55
Mushroom Walnut Pate 64
Oatmeal Sunflower Bread, 63
Raw Pecan Sushi with Tempura 166
Seitan
BBQ Noodles 197
Grilled "Chicken" Mexican Mole 59
Seitan Loaf 111

Sesame Oil
Marinated Baked Tofu Salad 173
Marinated Tofu Salad 67
Mushroom Pho 183
Mushroom Stroganoff 220
Pot Stickers 35
Raw Pecan Sushi with Tempura 166
Saag Paneer 237
Sea Palm Strudel 51
Stuffed Mushrooms 145
Vietnamese Summer Rolls 66

Soy-free
Balsamic Vinaigrette 102
Butternut Squash Soup 96
Caramelized Brussels Sprouts 94
Carrot Chipotle Pate 236
Coconut Oil Pie Crust 68
Fiddlehead and Potato Curry 172
Green Smoothie 29
Kofta Balls in Tomato Sauce 209
Le Fricot 139
Lemon Tahini Spread 233
Marinated Baked Tofu Salad 173
Mid-East Lentils and Rice 65
Mixed Vegetable Kurma 211
Mushroom Pho 183
Pastrami Spiced Young Carrots 192
Raw Beanless Hummus 105
Raw Curried Samosas 123
Raw Fresh Herb Cashew Pate 222
Raw Kale Salad 90
Raw Key Lime Pie 152
Raw Mock Tuna Salad 155
Raw Nori Wrap 106
Raw Pecan Sushi with Tempura 166
Raw Stuffed Avocado 89
Raw Three Berry Pie 156
Red Lentil Hummus 101
Roasted Garlic 136
Samosas 202
Sour Crème & Onion Kale Chips 30
Strawberry Blonde Smoothie 24
Tabouli 160
The Sufi Poet 100
Tomato Basil Coulee 134
Vegan Bolognese Sauce 140
Wild Raw Tomato Soup 19
Yellow Mung Dal Soup 213

Soy Milk
Banana Crème Pie 14
Carrot Cake 84
Ranch Dressing 218

Squash
Butternut Squash Soup 96
Harvest Vegetable Platter, 55
Roasted Kabocha Squash Salad 37
Spaghetti Squash Cakes 86

Stuffing
Harvest Vegetable Platter, 55

Tahini
Lemon Tahini Spread 233
Raw Beanless Hummus 105
Raw Nori Wrap 106
Red Lentil Hummus 101
Super Grain Salad with Fakin' Bacon and
Lemon Tahini Dressing 185

Tempeh
Asian Long Bean and Tempeh Salad 36
Pot Stickers 35
Super Grain Salad with Fakin' Bacon and
Lemon Tahini Dressing 185
Tempeh and Vegetable Hash 234
Tempeh Bourguignon 122

Textured Vegetable Protein (TVP)
Lone Star Vegan Chili 217
Summer Rolls 200
Vegan Bolognese Sauce 140

Tofu
Braised Tofu with Quinoa 129
Chocolate Orange Mousse Pie 115
Chocolate Tart 50
Curry Apple Tofu 10
Grilled "Chicken" Mexican Mole 59
Hoppin' John Fritters 227
Marinated Baked Tofu Salad 173
Marinated Tofu Salad 67
Mushroom Walnut Pate 64
Picadillo Vegetarian 221
Pot Stickers 35
Quinoa Tabouli 149

Tofu
Saag Paneer 237
Spinach Mushroom Loaf 133
Summer Rolls 200
Taza Chocolate Cheesecake 109
Tomato Delight 9
Vietnamese Summer Rolls 66
Wild Mushroom Tofu Scramble 180

Tomato Dishes
Grilled "Chicken" Mexican Mole 59
Kofta Balls in Tomato Sauce 209
Lone Star Vegan Chili 217
Raw Tortilla Soup 26
Smokey Tomato Aioli 135
Tomato Basil Coulee 134
Tomato Delight 9
Wild Raw Tomato Soup 19

Vermicelli
BBQ Noodles 197
Tomato Delight 9
Vietnamese Summer Rolls 66

Walnuts
Brownies, 46
Carrot Cake 84
Chocolate tart 50
Mushroom Walnut Pate 64
Raw Mock Tuna Salad 155

Wasabi
Sea Palm Strudel 51

Wraps
Raw Nori Wrap 106
Yogi Wraps 21